CAROLINA WHITEWATER
A Canoeist's Guide
to the Western Carolinas

Other Menasha Ridge Guides

Northern Georgia Canoeing, Bob Sehlinger and Don Otey

Southern Georgia Canoeing, Bob Sehlinger and Don Otey

A Canoeing and Kayaking Guide to the Streams of Tennessee,
Bob Sehlinger and Bob Lantz

A Canoeing and Kayaking Guide to the Streams of Kentucky
by Bob Sehlinger

Wild Water West Virginia, Paul Davidson and Bob Burrell

Whitewater Home Companion, Southeastern Rivers,
Volume I, William Nealy

CAROLINA WHITEWATER

A Canoeist's Guide to the Western Carolinas

FOURTH EDITION

Bob Benner

MENASHA RIDGE PRESS

Hillsborough
North Carolina

Table of Contents

PART 1

Introduction   3
Carolina Overview   5
  Clubs and Organizations   8
  North Carolina Natural and Scenic Rivers   12
  State Water Trails   12
Paddler Information   13
  Rating the Paddler   13
  Winter Canoeing   19
  Legal Rights of the Canoeist   21
  Safety   22
  Explanation   24

PART 2

Section 1   29

  Alarka Creek   31 □ Caney Fork Creek   33 □ Cullasaja River 35 □
  Deep Creek   36 □ Hiawassee River   39 □ Jonathans Creek   41 □
  Little Tennessee River   44 □ Nantahala River   47 □ Oconalufftee
  River   49 □ Pigeon River   51 □ Pigeon River, East Fork   55 □
  Pigeon River, West Fork   57 □ Raven Fork River   58 □ Soco Creek
  60 □ Tuckaseigee River   63 □ Tusquitee Creek   69

Section 2   70
  Big Laurel Creek   71 □ Broad River 73 □ Davidson River   75 □
  First Broad River   76 □ French Broad   79 □ French Broad, North
  Fork   88 □ Green River   91 □ Swannanoa River   95

Section 3   99

Buck Creek   101 □   Buffalo Creek   103 □   Catawba River   105 □
Catawba River, North Fork   108 □   Henry Fork River   111 □   Jacob
Fork River   115 □   Johns River   117 □   New River   121 □   North Fork,
New River   125 □   South Fork, New River   129 □   Nolichucky
River   135 □   North Toe River and Toe River   139 □   South Toe
River   145 □   South Yadkin River   149 □   Upper Creek   155 □
Uwharrie River   157 □   Watauga River   161 □   Wilson
Creek   167

Section 4   169

Dan River   171 □   Elk Creek   175 □   Fisher River   176 □   Lewis
Fork, North Prong   178 □   Lewis Fork, South Prong   180 □   Little
River   181 □   Mayo River, North Fork   184 □   Mayo River, South
Fork   186 □   Mitchell River   189 □   Reddies River   191 □   Stony
Fork Creek   193 □   Yadkin River   195

Section 5   197

Chattooga River   199 □   Chauga River, S.C.   207 □   Doe River   209
□   Elk River   213 □   Haw River   215 □   North Tyger and Tyger River   219
□   South Tyger River, S.C.   221

Section 6   222

Introduction   223 □   Broad River, North and South Carolina   225 □
Enoree River, South Carolina   237 □   Tyger River, South Carolina   241

Suggested Reading   247
Index   251

Acknowledgements

The author would like to acknowledge the many people whose assistance made such an undertaking possible. There are so many, too numerous to mention, who have lent a helping hand in some way or another. A few whose efforts require a special note of thanks are:

Steve Erikson, Buddy Rockett, and Dale Erikson for their time in previewing the original work in progress; and Steve and Tom Erikson for their willingness to chase the wild goose over the years.

Ed Gertler and Bob Loddengaard for their notes on the Watauga and the Haw, respectively, and to Tommy McNabb for his assistance on the Dan River.

Dr. Gordon Howard for his work and help on water flow on the Chattooga.

Harry Lewis for his invaluable information on stream flow in the Tennessee Valley and to T.V.A. for their support in providing such information.

And last, but certainly not least, all of the many friends who joined in "interesting" exploratory trips and who undoubtedly questioned the advisability of that friendship at times when such trips turned into hikes down dry streambeds; sometimes into ice breakers; and sometimes into major engineering feats; but always into memorable outings.

Part 1

Part I

Introduction

This guide has been written for the use of the recreational open boater who prefers his cruising type craft to the decked canoes and kayaks. Much of the water included is suitable for novice paddling; however, some of it will test the skills of the advanced deck boat paddler. The fact that it is primarily directed toward the open boater should be kept in mind when referring to the rapid classification system as used here. It is quite difficult to class a rapid and remain totally objective because that judgement is generally relative to one's experience. In any case it is hoped that the system will be found to be consistent.

As the sport of canoeing grows one sees more and more clubs being organized with canoeing as their main interest. Some long time paddlers question the need for such growth or organization and rightly so, but this is one of the few safe proving grounds available for aspiring canoeists. It is primarily through clubs that one can obtain competent instruction toward improving skills and learning safe canoeing practices. Also, it is only by organization that our free flowing rivers are going to be saved for future generations.

Information on safety has been included because of the certain hazards involved in the sport. Hopefully the suggestions made will lessen the possibilities of accidents other than normal swampings and dunkings that are likely to occur.

Along with these suggestions are rules which will be helpful for the canoeist who decides that Labor Day shouldn't necessarily mean the end of his season. More and more paddlers are venturing forth in the middle of winter to experience a completely different world. The risks increase as the air and water temperatures decrease. A familiarity with certain facts relating to exposure can cut down considerably on these inherent risks.

The average canoeist in North Carolina seems to harbor the idea that he has an inalienable right to paddle on any stream that has enough water to float his canoe. This most certainly is a misconception under present interpretation of state law and an attempt to clarify what the rights of the canoeist may be is discussed.

An explanation of the overall format has been included so that the reader can fully understand the organization of the materials on the streams and the various sections that it may be divided into. In "Canoeing White Water," Randy Carter established such an understandable outline in describing rivers that the author has followed it rather closely.

Finally, the major organization of the book contains six sections on rivers. The first four consist of groups of rivers in neighboring counties in the foothills and mountains of the state. The fifth section contains the Chattooga, the Chauga, the Doe and the Elk, which are located in neighboring states. The Haw River, a stream of the Piedmont, has been included due to its extreme popularity. The last section has very little whitewater. It has been included to offer the paddler a selection of some 200 miles suitable for camping trips.

The maps of the various streams in each section are drawn to scale. Scale: 1″ = 2 miles.

The original reason for undertaking such a work as this was to provide a source of information for those who would like to take their pleasure in paddling the many beautiful rivers of Western Carolina. The effort will have been worthwhile if any small portion of the great pleasure the author has experienced on the several hundred miles contained herein is imparted to the reader.

Carolina Overview

 Physiologically, North and South Carolina are sisters. Both are bordered on the west by the Blue Ridge Mountains and on the east by the Atlantic Ocean. Moving west to east in either state, three major physiographic regions are encountered: The Blue Ridge Mountains, the Piedmont, and the Coastal Plain. In both states the coastal plain is locally referred to as the "lowlands," while the Piedmont and Mountain regions are collectively known as "uplands" or "highlands."

The Blue Ridge Mountains are the eastern part of the Appalachian Mountain System, extending from Southeastern Pennsylvania across Maryland, Virginia, North Carolina, South Carolina and Northern Georgia. In North Carolina, the Blue Ridge forms the eastern section of a mountain chain more than seventy-five miles wide, where cross ridges connect the more westerly Black Mountains and Great Smokies. In this area, known as the "Land of the Sky," are forty three peaks of over 6,000 feet, and 125 others of more than 5,000 feet. Mountain valleys here are characteristically narrow, deep, and densely forested with elevations consistently above 2,000 feet.

By contrast, Western South Carolina extends only slightly into the Blue Ridge Mountains, where a small number of peaks not exceeding 3,600 feet rise rather abruptly from the foothills. Where mountains occupy approximately 6,000 square miles in North Carolina, there are only about 500 square miles of mountain terrain in South Carolina. The highest point in South Carolina is Sassafrass Mountain (3,560 feet), situated on the North Carolina/South Carolina state line.

The coolest and wettest portion of both states, the Blue Ridge Mountain region is not farmed extensively nor densely populated, with the steepness of the terrain making the land more suitable for forest than for farms.

Geologically, the region is underlain by "crystalline" rocks such as granite, slate, and gneiss, which are dense and hard. The mountains are usually steep with V-shaped valleys. Slopes are covered with thick soil and luxurious forests which retard run-off.

Many rivers are born high in the mountains of the Carolinas, flowing down in all directions like chocolate on a sundae. Typically running along steep, rocky channels, the streams roll swiftly down the mountains over an abundance of rapids and falls, broadening when they reach the valley floors. West of the Blue Ridge the streams flow north and west, forming a major part of the Tennessee River Drainage. To the north are the headwaters of the New, which eventually empties into the Ohio. On the southeastern slopes of the Blue Ridge the Broad, Catawba, and Yadkin are born. These merge with other drainages after crossing into South Carolina and finally find their way to the Atlantic Ocean. To the south are the headwaters of the Savannah River, which follows the South Carolina/Georgia border to the sea.

Beyond the Blue Ridge to the east the Carolinas drop out of the mountains and out onto the rolling plateau of the Piedmont. Extending from the Blue Ridge Escarpment to the fall line where the topography suddenly drops off onto the flat expanse of the Coastal Plain, the Piedmont descends at roughly 3.5 ft. per mile with the terrain changing gradually from rolling hills to flat upland. Deeply cut by rivers and creeks, the hills of the Piedmont rise from 400 to 1,500 feet above sea level. Though the Piedmont is underlain by the same crystalline rock as the Blue Ridge region, it lacks the mountains' high relief. Only occasionally are the rolling plains punctuated by a prominent hill. Comprising about forty percent of the area of both Carolinas, the Piedmont is generally well developed and populated. Rivers flowing through the Piedmont, while lacking the high gradient and pristine setting of the mountains, are generally attractive and some are endowed with a variety of rapids and falls.

The Coastal Plain region of the Carolinas begins at the fall line, where the underlying geology abruptly changes from hard crystalline rock to sandy loam over marl. Known locally as the "low country," the plain was at the bottom of the Atlantic Ocean in the past geologic ages. The Fall Line, where a dramatic drop in elevation occurs as one moves east from the Piedmont into the Coastal Plain, runs very roughly on the line of Falls-of-the-Roanoke to Durham to Columbia to Augusta (Ga.). Near the Fall Line the Coastal Plain consists of small hills. Moving toward the ocean, the terrain flattens. Swamp and marsh characterize the coastline corridor to the far east with many natural lakes occurring. Below the mouth of the Cape Fear River the coastal environs assume a more tropical look with black water (caused by tannic acid from decaying vegetation), thick groves of palmettos, magnolias, tall cypress draped with Spanish Moss, and live oak.

The Carolinas are alive with beautiful and diverse flora and fauna. Because of their great variety of climate and soil they have the greatest variety of plant life of any area in the Eastern U.S. Longleaf pine dominates the upper coastal plain along with water oaks, and hickories. In the Piedmont, pine remains plentiful but hardwood forests are the order of the day with deciduous oak being most prevalent followed by beech, birch, ash, maple, black walnut, sycamore, and yellow poplar. On the mountains the forest is generally comprised of oak, chestnut, laurel, white pine, and hemlock. Wildlife is abundant and varied, especially birds, many of which winter and breed in the coastal marshes.

Climate in the Carolinas is equable and pleasant, being cool in the mountains and almost subtropical on the Coastal Plain with the Piedmont representing the middle of the spectrum. Temperatures average approximately 10 degrees cooler in the mountains than in the low country. The mean annual temperature for North Carolina is about 59 degrees and for South Carolina 63 degrees, with January being the coldest month and July the warmest. North Carolina receives more rain than South Carolina owing to its larger mountain region. Averages for both states approximate fifty-four inches in the mountains, forty-seven inches in the Piedmont, and forty-eight inches in the Coastal Plain. On the east slope of some of the mountains the precipitation is exceptionally heavy. Heavy snow is unusual except in the mountains. Winds are variable and seldom violent except during the storms of fall along the coast.

Clubs and Organizations

There are a number of local and national organizations that the paddler should be aware of. We have attempted to list those groups that we are acquainted with that are active in the surrounding area.

Most local clubs have as their main objectives the training of members toward safer canoeing, and the preservation of the streams on which they paddle. Generally they have regularly scheduled trips throughout most of the year and periodically publish newsletters which are in themselves a valuable source of information for the canoeist.

For those who wish to improve their skills in the canoe it is almost a necessity to paddle with those of greater experience. In many areas "the local club" will be the only source of such experience.

Many of us begin paddling to get away from the hustle and bustle of today's busy life; to get back to nature; to see things that few others see; or to engage in an activity that few people do. For this reason joining a club and participating in organized trips might seem alien to us. However, the fact remains, without organizations that are willing to work and fight toward preserving our free flowing streams, there may be none to enjoy in the future. We don't care to see our rivers become the "L.A. Freeway" at rush hour, but can we afford to be so selfish as to want to keep our favorite streams all to ourselves? How much weight will a handful carry when the "Corps" begins surveying for the best damsite? Your "bag" may be an occasional quiet float trip down your favorite stream with one or two close friends, but we hope you will see fit to support the organization in your area that may help you save that stream some day. We can save our rivers only if our numbers are large and we are well organized. Not quantity alone, but quantity with quality will be needed.

Local and Area

Carolina Canoe Club
P.O. Box 9011
Greensboro, N.C. 27408

Club made up primarily of cruising canoeists with membership over most of the state of North Carolina. Conduct regularly scheduled one and/or two day trips year round, stress safety, education and conservation. Dues $11.00/year.

Blue Ridge Canoe Club
P.O. Box 1938
Morganton, N.C. 28655

Dues $3.00/year.

Foothills Canoe Club
Rt. 2, Box 281
Mooresboro, N.C. 28114

Piedmont Paddlers
P.O. Box 11526
Charlotte, N.C. 28220

Initiation fee: $5.00; Dues: $7.50 individual, $10.00 family.

Coastal Canoeists
P.O. Box 566
Richmond, VA 23204

Don't let their name fool you. They cover the state of Virginia and surrounding states running the mountain streams as well as an occasional coastal river Dues. $8.00/year.

Float Fishermen of Virginia
Richard Abeyta, Treasurer
417 Beauregard Ave.
Petersburg, VA 23803

Dues: $10.00. Active paddlers, fishermen and conservationists. Chapters all over the state.

Georgia Canoeing Association
P.O. Box 7023
Atlanta, GA 30309

Dues: $7.50, which includes a guidebook and roster of members.

East Tennessee Whitewater Club
P.O. Box 3074
Oak Ridge, TN 37830

Dues: $3.00.

Tennessee Scenic Rivers Association
P.O. Box 3104
Nashville, TN 37219

Dues for first year: $5.00; continuing: $8.00.

Tennessee Valley Canoe Club
P.O. Box 1125
Chattanooga, TN 37401

Dues: $7.00.

National

American Whitewater Affiliation
P.O. Box 1483
Hagerstown, Maryland 21740

Composed of boating clubs and individuals interested in white water paddling. It promotes conservation, cruising, and wild water and slalom competition on national and international levels. "American Whitewater," the journal of the Affiliation, is published six times yearly. Dues $6.00/year.

American Canoe Association
4260 East Evans Avenue
Denver, Coloraro 80222

Comprised of individual members and clubs organized into regional divisions. The ACA conducts canoe and kayak cruises, promotes canoe sailing, encourages and sactions competition, and has conservation as one of its prime areas of interest. "Canoe," the official magazine, is published six times a year. Dues: $15.00, Magazine Subscription Rate: $20.00.

Conservation Organizations

We are losing our free flowing rivers and streams one by one in the frantic push for development. Whether that development be by damming, channelization or dredging, many miles of wild wonderful water will soon be lost forever. One of our most precious resources is literally going down the drain slowly but surely. We all must stand up and be heard if we are to stem the tide and save some of these waters for our future generations to know and enjoy.

There are many national and local organizations that have as one of their primary objectives the preservation of free flowing waters. We list only a few of these in hopes the reader might see fit to join in and support the cause.

American Rivers Conservation Council
324 C Street, S.E.
Washington, D.C. 20003

Founded in 1973, the American Rivers Conservation Council publishes a quarterly newsletter which contains articles about recent action in Congress dealing with wild and scenic rivers and with water resource projects. Also covered are the progress of wild and scenic river studies being performed by federal agencies and state scenic river programs.

In addition to reporting on current events, the newsletter gives suggestions on how individuals can take action to help protect rivers.

Student membership: $5.00, Regular: $10.00, Founding: $25.00.

Conservation Council of North Carolina
P.O. Box 553
Carrboro, N.C. 27510

The Conservation Council of North Carolina is a statewide organization which coordinates activities of the many conservation groups within North Carolina. A monthly newsletter is published commenting on the various environmental concerns in the state. Among the many special committees of CCNC is the River Preservation Committee.

Student Membership: $5.00, Individual: $10.00, Family: $15.00, Organization: $20.00.

Joseph LeConte Chapter Sierra Club
4217 Laurel Ridge Road
Raleigh, N.C. 27612

The LeConte Chapter is composed of Sierra Club members in North Carolina and currently has active groups within the chapter in most of the major population areas of the state. Most of the groups have some canoeing activities going on through the year.

■

Exertion brings vital physiological reactions when there are worthwhile goals to achieve. Without weariness there can be no real appreciation of rest, without hunger no enjoyment of food, without the ancient responses to the harsh simplicities of the environment that shaped mankind, a man cannot know the urges within him. Having known this during a period of life when I could satisfy the needs, I think I understand what wilderness can mean to the young men of today. Sigurd F. Olson

North Carolina Natural and Scenic Rivers

A Natural and Scenic Rivers System was created by the General Assembly in 1971 to preserve and protect certain free flowing rivers in their natural state. A thirteen mile segment of the Linville River and some 26.5 miles of the New and the South Fork of the New became the first rivers to be included in the system in 1976. Currently, the state is treading lightly around the troubled waters of establishing scenic rivers. Opposition, primarily from land owners, has arisen in every case that has come up for study in the recent past. However, progress is being made toward studying the Dan for inclusion in either the state or federal system.

Information regarding trips on these streams can be quite useful. Such information as: date of trip, put in and take out, length of trip (time and distance), number of participants, and anything unusual can prove important. Jot it down on a card and send it to the author in care of Pisgah Providers. Such reports will be tabulated and forwarded to the North Carolina Department of Natural Resources and Community Development. This type of data can be most helpful in making decisions on these streams.

State Water Trails

In 1973 a state trails committee was established by the General Assembly to represent the citizen's trail interests. Included in the area are trails for hikers, O.R.V.'s, horseback riders, bicyclists, and canoeists. Out of this committee and from interest by the North Carolina Department of Natural Resources and Community Development has grown the North Carolina Trails Association. This organization, still somewhat in the embryo stage, is composed of individuals and groups interested in the promotion of trails and trail related activities. In 1978 some 62 miles of the Lumber River received recognition as the state's first water trail. Also a stretch of the French Broad received such recognition later that year. In addition to these, approximately 1,400 miles of other streams and lakes are deemed to have·potential for establishment as State Water Trails.

If interested in working toward a better system of trails in North Carolina contact:

North Carolina Trails Association
P.O. Box 1033
Greensboro, NC 27402

Paddler Information

The most widely publicized of the *paddler* self-evaluations was created by the Keel-Haulers Canoe Club of Ohio. This system brings the problem of matching paddlers with rivers into perspective but seems to overemphasize nonpaddling skills. A canoe clinic student who is athletically inclined but almost totally without paddling skill once achieved a rating of 15 points using the Keel-Haulers system. His rating, based almost exclusively on general fitness and strength, incorrectly implied that he was capable of handling many Class II and Class III rivers. A second problem evident in the system is the lack of depth in skill category descriptions. Finally, confusion exists in several rating areas as to whether the evaluation applies to open canoes, decked canoes, or both.

To remedy these perceived shortcomings and to bring added objectivity to paddler self-evaluation, Bob Sehlinger* has attempted to refine the paddler rating system. Admittedly the refined system is more complex and exhaustive, but not more so than warranted by the situation. Heavy emphasis is placed on paddling skills, with description adopted from several different evaluation formats, including a non-numerical system proposed by Dick Schwind.**

 * Sehlinger, Bob; *A Canoeing and Kayaking Guide to the Streams of Tennessee*, Thomas Press.
** Schwind, Dick; "Rating Systems for Boating Difficulty," *American Whitewater Journal*, Volume 20, Number 3, May/June 1975.

Rating the Paddler

Instructions: All items, except the first, carry points that may be added to obtain an overall rating. All items except "Rolling Ability" apply to both open and decked boats. Rate open and decked boat skills separately.

---

1. Prerequisite Skills. Before paddling on moving current, the paddler should:
- a. Have some swimming ability.
- b. Be able to paddle instinctively on nonmoving water (lake). (This presumes knowledge of basic strokes.)
- c. Be able to guide and control the canoe from either side without changing paddling sides.
- d. Be able to guide and control the canoe (or kayak) while paddling backwards.

e. Be able to move the canoe (or kayak) laterally.

f. Understand the limitations of the boat.

g. Be practiced in "wet exit" if in a decked boat.

2. Equipment. Award points on the suitability of your equipment to white-water. Whether you own, borrow, or rent the equipment makes no difference. *Do not* award points for both *Open Canoe* and *Decked Boat.*

Open Canoe

0 Points: Any canoe less than 15 ft. for tandem; any canoe less than 14 ft. for solo.

1 Point: Canoe with moderate rocker, full depth, and recurved bow; should be 15 ft. or more in length for tandem and 14 ft. or more in length for solo and have bow and stern painters.

2 Points: Whitewater canoe. Strong rocker design, full bow with recurve, full depth amidships, no keel; meets or exceeds minimum length requirements as described under "1 Point"; made of hand-laid fiberglass, Kevlar, Marlex, or ABS *Royalex;* has bow and stern painters. Canoe as described under "1 Point" but with extra flotation.

3 Points: Canoe as described under "2 Points" but with extra flotation.

Decked Boat (K-1, K-2, C-1, C-2)

0 Points: Any decked boat lacking full flotation, spray skirt, or foot braces.

1 Point: Any fully equipped, decked boat with a wooden frame.

2 Points: Decked boat with full flotation, spray skirt and foot braces; has grab loops; made of hand-laid fiberglass, Marlex, or Kevlar.

3 Points: Decked boat with foam wall reinforcement and split flotation; Neoprene spray skirt; boat has knee braces, foot braces, and grab loops; made of hand-laid fiberglass or Kevlar only.

■

This earth is something you protect every day of the year. A river is something you defend every inch of its course.

James A. Michener, *from* Centennial

Table 1: Rating the River

Points	Secondary Factors — Factors Related Primarily to Success in Negotiating		Primary Factors — Factors Affecting Both Success and Safety				Secondary Factors — Factors Related Primarily to Safe Rescue				
	Obstacles, rocks and trees	Waves	Turbulence	Bends	Length (feet)	Gradient (feet/mile)	Resting or rescue spots	Water Velocity (mph)	Width and depth	Temp. (F)	Accessibility
0	None	Few inches high, avoidable	None	Few, very gradual	<100	<5, regular slope	Almost anywhere	<3	Narrow (<75 feet), and shallow <3 feet	>65	Road along river
1	Few, passage almost straight through	Low (up to 1 ft.) regular, avoidable	Minor eddies	Many, gradual gradual	100-700	5-15, regular slope		3-6	Wide (>75 feet), and shallow (<3 feet)	55-65	<1 hour travel by foot or water
2	Courses easily recognizable	Low to med. (up to 3 ft.) regular, avoidable	Medium eddies	Few, sharp, blind. Scouting necessary	700-5,000	15-40, ledges or steep drops		6-10	Narrow (<75 feet) and deep (>3 feet)	45-55	1 hour to 1 day travel by foot or water
3	Maneuvering, course not easily recognizable avoidable	Med. to large (up to 5 ft.), mostly regular,	Strong eddies and cross		>500	>40, steep drops, small falls	A good one below every danger spot	>10 or flood	Wide (>75 feet) and deep (>3 ft.)	<45	>1 day travel by foot or water
4	Intricate maneuvering, course hard to recognize large, unavoidable	Large, irregular, avoidable or med. to cross currents	Very strong eddies, strong								
5	Course tortuous, frequent scouting	Large, irregular, unavoidable	Large scale eddies and cross currents, some up and down								
6	Very tortuous; always scout from shore	Very large (>5 ft.), irregular, unavoidable, special equipment required						Almost none			

Source: Prepared by Guidebook Committee—AWA (From "American White Water," Winter, 1957.)

NOTE: RATING | APPROXIMATE DIFFICULTY

I   Easy
II   Requires Care
III   Difficult
IV   Very Difficult
V   Exceedingly Difficult
VI   Utmost Difficulty–Near Limit of Navigability

TOTAL POINTS (from above)	APPROXIMATE SKILL REQUIRED
0-7	Practiced Beginner
8-14	Intermediate
15-21	Experienced
22-28	Highly Skilled (Several years with organized group)
29-35	Team of Experts

3. Experience. Compute the following to determine *preliminary points,* then convert the preliminary points to *final points* according to the conversion table.

Conversion Table

Preliminary Points	Final Points
0-20	0
21-60	1
61-100	2
101-200	3
201-300	4
301-up	5

Note: This is the only evaluation item where it is possible to accrue more than 3 points.

Number of days spent each year paddling

Class I rivers	× 1 =	_____
Class II rivers	× 2 =	_____
Class III rivers	× 3 =	_____
Class IV rivers	× 4 =	_____
Class V rivers	× 5 =	_____

Preliminary   Points Subtotal   _____

Number of years paddling

experience _____ × subtotal   =

Total Preliminary Points   _____

4. Swimming
0 Points: Cannot swim
1 Point: Weak swimmer
2 Points: Average swimmer
3 Points: Strong swimmer (competition level or skin diver)

5. Stamina
0 Points: Cannot run mile in less than 10 minutes
1 Point: Can run a mile in 7 to 10 minutes
2 Points: Can run a mile in less than 7 minutes

6. Upper Body Strength
0 Points: Cannot do 15 push-ups
1 Point: Can do 16 to 25 pushups
2 Points: Can do more than 25 push-ups

7. Boat Control

0 Points:	Can keep boat fairly straight
1 Point:	Can maneuver in moving water; can avoid big obstacles
2 Points:	Can maneuver in heavy water; knows how to work with the current
3 Points:	Finesse in boat placement in all types of water, uses current to maximum advantage

8. Aggressiveness

0 Points:	Does not play or work river at all
1 Point:	Timid; plays a little on familiar streams
2 Points:	Plays a lot; works most rivers hard
3 Points:	Plays in heavy water with grace and confidence

9. Eddy Turns

0 Points:	Has difficulty making eddy turns from moderate current
1 Point:	Can made eddy turns in either direction from moderate current; can enter moderate current from eddy
2 Points:	Can catch medium eddies in either direction from heavy current; can enter very swift current from eddy
3 Points:	Can catch small eddies in heavy current

10. Ferrying

0 Points:	Cannot ferry
1 Point:	Can ferry upstream and downstream in *moderate* current
2 Points:	Can ferry upstream in *heavy* current; can ferry downstream in *moderate* current
3 Points:	Can ferry upstream and downstream in *heavy* current

11. Water Reading

0 Points:	Often in error
1 Point:	Can plan route in short rapid with several well-spaced obstacles
2 Points:	Can confidently run lead in continuous Class II; can predict the effects of waves and holes on boat
3 Points:	Can confidently run lead in continuous Class III; has knowledge to predict and handle the effects of reversals, side currents, and turning drops

12. Judgement

0 Points:	Often in error
1 Point:	Has average ability to analyze difficulty of rapids

18

| 2 Points: | Has good ability to analyze difficulty of rapids and make independent judgements as to which should not be run |
| 3 Points: | Has the ability to assist fellow paddlers in evaluating the difficulty of rapids; can explain subtleties to paddlers with less experience |

13. Bracing

0 Points:	Has difficulty bracing in Class II rivers
1 Point:	Can correctly execute bracing strokes in Class II water
2 Points:	Can correctly brace in intermittent whitewater with medium waves and vertical drops of 3 ft. or less
3 Points:	Can brace effectively in continuous whitewater with large waves and large vertical drops (4 ft. and up)

14. Rescue Ability

0 Points:	Self-rescue in flatwater
1 Point:	Self-rescue in mild whitewater
2 Points:	Self-rescue in Class III; can assist others in mild whitewater
3 Points:	Can assist others in heavy whitewater

15. Rolling Ability

0 Points:	Can only roll in pool
1 Point:	Can roll 3 out of 4 times in moving current
2 Points:	Can roll 3 out of 4 times in Class II whitewater
3 Points:	Can roll 4 out of 5 times in Class III and IV whitewater

Winter Canoeing

Winter canoeing can be beautiful but it also can be quite dangerous unless certain precautions are taken. Some rules that should be followed by open boaters are:

1. Canoe those streams on which you can walk to shore at any point. It is best to stay off the larger rivers and those even nearing flood stage.
2. Always have at least three canoes in the party.
3. Everyone should have a *complete* change of clothing in a waterproof container that will withstand pressures of immersion.
4. Each participant should carry on his person a supply of matches in a waterproof container.
5. Remember that the classification of any particular river is automatically upgraded when canoeing in cold weather. This is due to the extreme effects on the body upon immersion in cold water.

Cold Weather Survival

With more and more paddlers going out in cold weather to engage in their sport a basic knowledge in cold water and cold weather survival is necessary.

When immersed in water the loss of heat from the body becomes much more rapid and survival times without suitable clothing in cold water become very short. For instance, wet clothes lose about 90 percent of their insulating value, and can cause heat loss 240 times faster than dry clothing.

The following table gives the approximate survival times of humans immersed in water at various temperatures.

Water Temp. F.	Exhaustion or Unconsciousness	Survival Time
32.5	Less than 15 min.	Less than 15-45 min.
32.5-40	15-30 min.	30-90 min.
40-50	30-60 min.	1-3 hrs.
50-60	1-2 hrs.	1-6 hrs.
60-70	2-7 hrs.	2-40 hrs.
70-80	3-12 hrs.	3 hrs.-indefinite

The greatest change in survival time occurs as the water temperature drops below 50°F.

Swimming in cold water increases the flow of water past the body and pumps heat out of the clothing so that in spite of heat production the body loses heat more rapidly. If there is no prospect of getting out of the water immediately, survival time will be longer if one does not swim but relies on his life jacket to hold him up. Better still, assume the HELP position (Heat Escape Lessening Position) in which the knees are tucked close to the chest. This allows one to retain body heat longer. It is, therefore, imperative that a life jacket with adequate flotation be worn. Swim only if there is danger downstream.

Wool along with waterproof outerware (rain suit) is highly recommended for cold weather paddling. Wool has the unique ability to provide warmth even when wet and to dry from within, thus wicking moisture away. Even better than wool is the wet suit, which is an absolute necessity for those who paddle decked boats. Also, a wool hat can help tremendously in preserving body heat since a great deal of heat is lost through an unprotected head or neck.

Dry clothing should definitely be carried in a waterproof bag on all winter trips and changed into if one gets wet. Quite often you must insist that the victim change clothing and render assistance in changing because of his lack of coordination. The victim more than likely will be totally unaware of his poor reactions.

Symptoms of exposure occur generally as follows: uncontrollable shivering; vague, slow, slurred speech; memory lapses; slowing of reactions, fumbling hands, and apparent exhaustion. Unconsciousness will follow and then death. The mental effects will be similar to those observed in states of extreme fatigue.

In cases of extreme exposure build a fire, give the victim a warm drink, if he is able to swallow; strip him and put him into a sleeping bag with another person who is also stripped. *Remember* that the victim must be warmed from an outside heat source since he cannot generate his own body heat. *Do not* give the victim any form of alcohol.

■

It is difficult to find in life any event which so effectually condenses intense nervous sensation into the shortest possible space of time as does the work of shooting, or running an immense rapid. There is no toil, no heart breaking labour about it, but as much coolness, dexterity, and skill as man can throw into the work of hand, eye, and head; knowledge of when to strike and how to do it; knowledge of water and rock, and of the one hundred combinations which rock and water can assume . . .

Sir William Francis Butler (1872)

Legal Rights of the Canoeist

In any discussion of the legal rights of canoeists the question of navigability arises. It is generally assumed that if a stream is navigable one has the legal right to float a canoe on it. Basically this is correct in the state of North Carolina.

However, the question remains as to what constitutes "navigability" under the laws of the state. One old case defined a stream which loggers used to float their timber down to be navigable; but it is believed that this case defined a limited type of navigable purpose. The general idea seems to be that if a waterway is suitable as a "highway" of commerce it is navigable and the public has a right to use it. When a navigable stream crosses an owner's land the state owns the bottom and the owner cannot legally block use of the stream for navigation or fishing.

In a recent decision, when a land owner attempted to block a waterway, declaring it non-navigable, the California Court of Appeals determined that the test of navigability is met if the stream is capable of boating for pleasure. In making his decision the judge pointed out that the streams of California are a vital recreational resource of the state. Perhaps this case may set a precedent that will be followed in the future in determining the right of the canoeist. Although with the strong laws protecting the property rights of the individual owner in North Carolina this may never be pertinent.

When a person owns land over which a "nonnavigable" stream flows, he owns the land under the stream and has the right to control the surface of the water. For this reason when canoeing on streams of questionable navigability, it is best to observe one's manners to the fullest. If you must cross private property for any reason request the owner's permission before doing so. Generally speaking, the land owner will be a reasonable person if approached courteously and respectfully. More often than not the unreasonable property owner is one whose property rights have been abused in the past.

With the popularity of canoeing growing tremendously, travel on our streams is increasing also. Prime examples of such heavy usage can be found already on the Nantahala and the Chattooga. Be sure that you aren't the proverbial straw that breaks the camel's back by committing some careless act that might cause a landowner along a stream of questionable navigability to block access to it, or perhaps to take the next guy to court for trespass. Make sure that you leave the door open for the next guy.

Safety

A section on safety has been included because of the great interest in white water canoeing and rafting among the uninitiated. The fact is there are potential hazards involved in the sport which in many instances is the very reason many are attracted to it. However, with normal precautions and good judgement in determining one's level of skill it can be a safe sport under normal conditions.

A few tips for the paddler to follow to insure that his trip is an enjoyable one and above all a safe one, are listed. If each and every one of these rules is followed while on the river, you won't become the proverbial "accident looking for a place to happen."

1. Never boat alone. Three boats are generally considered a minimum on anything but small low water streams.

2. Always carry a life jacket. Wear it unless you are a capable swimmer and even then have it on when in water difficulit enough that there is any possibility of upset.

3. Know your ability and don't attempt water beyond this ability. In considering whether or not to run a particular rapid ask:
   a. Is it much greater in difficuilty than anything I've attempted before?
   b. If I try it and don't make it will I place others in a difficult or dangerous situation in order to rescue me or my boat?
If the answer to either one is yes, don't try it. No experienced paddler will ever accuse you of being "chicken" when you back off, but he will respect your good judgement.

4. Be adequately equipped. Have an extra paddle in the canoe, if not an extra one for each paddler. Have bow and stern lines 8-15 ft. long tied on securely to the ends of the craft.

Never tie the ends of these lines in the boat. At the same time be sure no lines are positioned so that they might entangle the canoeist's feet. The author observed a canoe swamp in Nantahala Falls which in itself was certainly not too unusual nor was it very dangerous. The paddler came in for what was a terrifying moment when he came up wearing his bailer line around his neck— with the other end still tied onto the boat. He simply had far too much line tied to his bailer.

A good standard First Aid Kit should be carried in a waterproof container, and a throw line at least 3/8 in. in size, 75-100 ft. long, preferably polypropylene, can become a necessity on all except the small shallow streams.

5. If traveling with a group, or club, know the plans of the group, the organization of the trip, and follow the decisions of the leader. Most clubs have standard trip rules established which determine the trip leader's responsibilities as well as those of each paddler individually.

One rule generally followed on the river is that each canoe is responsible for keeping the canoe following in sight. This same rule should apply when a caravan or cars are traveling to or from the put in or take out.

6. Scout unfamiliar rapids before running them. Even those that are familiar can change considerably at different water levels.

7. Stay off flooded streams. The great increase in drownings from canoeing and rafting accidents has resulted almost entirely from mishaps on swollen rivers.

8. Do not attempt to run dams or abrupt ledges. Quite often a hydraulic jump is formed in which the surface water flows back upstream, causing a rolling action. This rolling action tends to hold a boat or a person in, tumbling them around and around. The only escape is to swim out the end or get rid of your life jacket and dive toward the bottom into the downriver current.

9. If you spill, get to the upstream end of the boat and if possible, stay with it. Don't risk the possibility of being pinned against a rock. If others spill, rescue the boaters and then go after the boat and equipment.

10. If you get broadside on a rock or other obstacle, lean toward the obstacle—downstream from the direction of the current. It is the unnatural reaction, but the correct thing to do in order to prevent the upstream gunwhale from dipping into the current and swamping the boat.

In running smaller low water streams, the possibility of personal danger is usually not as great as in large volume rivers, but there are many things to watch for that might prove dangerous if not approached with caution. Some of the most common things that the paddler needs to beware of are logs and trees blocking the passage, barb wire fences which can prove difficult to see, and low water bridges which may be just high enough to lure the unwary paddler into attempting a run under them. If in doubt when approaching the latter, pull to shore well above it and check out the clearance. The American Whitewater Affiliation has a safety code which is quite inclusive and the aspiring boater should become familiar with the aspects of it.

Explanation

Description
A brief description of the stream as a whole or of the particular section is given.

Topographic Maps
"Topo Maps" are listed in the order in which the river flows. Unless otherwise noted all maps are located on the North Carolina Index. If there is not a local source for maps they are available on order from:
Branch of Distribution
U.S. Geological Survey
1200 South Eads Street
Arlington, Virginia 22202

Counties
Each stream will have the county in which a particular section is located, and where it flows through more than one they will be listed in the order in which the river flows.

Put In
The exact put in is listed, such as a particular highway or secondary road bridge. Where more than one section is listed, the put in for the following section will be the take out for the preceding section.

Gradient
The total gradient of a section has been given rather than breaking it down into an average number of feet per mile. This has been done since quite often on a long stretch the gradient might be rather great in one portion and not on another. Where the drop is quite rapid it will be listed as (1@40') which indicates one mile in the section will drop at the rate of 40' within that mile.

Difficulty
This refers to the rating of difficulty of the rapids located within the particuliar section of the stream. The rating system used is based on that of the *International Scale for Grading the Difficulty of River Cruising Routes.*

International Scale for Grading the Difficulting of River Cruising Routes

Rating	River or Individual Rapids Characteristics	Approximate Minimum Experience Required
Smooth Water		
A	Pools, lakes, rivers with velocity under 2 m.p.h.	Beginner

B	Rivers, velocity 2-4 m.p.h.	Beginner with river instructions
C	Rivers, velocity above 4 m.p.h., (max. back paddling speed). May have some sharp bends or obstructions.	Instructed and practiced beginner

White Water

1	Easy—sand banks, bends without difficulty, occasional small rapids with waves regular and low. Correct course may be easy to find but care is needed with minor obstacles like pebble banks, fallen trees, etc., especially on narrow rivers. River speed less than hard back paddling speed.	Practiced beginner
2	Medium—fairly frequent but unobstructed rapids, usually with regular waves, easy eddies and easy bends. Course generally easy to recognize. River speeds occasionally exceeding hard back paddling speed.	Intermediate
3	Difficult—maneuvering in rapids necessary. Small falls, large irregular waves covering boat, numerous rapids. Main current may swing under bushes, branches, or overhangs. Course not always easily recognizable. Current speed usually less than fast forward paddling speed.	Experienced
4	Very Difficult—long extended stretches of rapids, high irregular waves with boulders directly in current. Difficult broken water, eddies and abrupt bends. Course often difficult to recognize and inspection from the bank frequently necessary. Swift current. Rough water experience indispensable.	Highly skilled (several years experience with organized group)
5	Exceedingly Difficuilt—long rocky rapids with difficult and completely irregular broken water which must be run head on. Very fast eddies, abrupt bends and vigorous cross currents. Difficult landings increase hazard. Frequent inspections necessary. Extensive experience necessary.	Team of experts
6	Limit of navigability—all previously mentioned difficulties increased to the limit. Only negotiable at favorable water levels. Cannot be attempted without risk of life.	Team of experts

It is important to know the difficulty rating of a particular river before setting out on it. The ratings used here are based on normal or ideal water heights.

The ratings will vary somewhat as the water level in the stream fluctuates.

The author has attempted to be as objective as possible in declaring whether or not a rapid is Class 3 or Class 4. Such a judgement will vary considerably from person to person according to his skill or experience.

Where a section has only one rapid of a higher difficulty than others it is listed 2-3/4, with the final number representing the one more difficuilt rapid as a Class 4.

Distance

Measured in miles from county and U.S.G.S. maps and generally rounded off.

Time

This is actual paddling time on the river including time for scouting when necessary. When paddling with a group larger than 2 or 3 canoes and when a lunch stop will be made additional time should be planned for.

Scenery

AA   Unusually beautiful even to the spectacular, generally remote and wild.

A   Generally remote and wild. Perhaps some signs of civilization but mostly uninhabited.

B   More pastoral type of country with more settled areas.

C   Fair amount of development, general signs of civilization such as garbage dumps, autos left on the side of the stream, visual pollution.

Water Quality

Excellent   Where water shed is protected and water generally remains "clear as crystal."

Good   Where some small amount of sediment appears but on the whole the water would be considered clean.

Fair   Heavier sediment in stream but no evident pollution.

Poor   Signs of human or industrial pollution to the extent water is actually discolored.

Gage

Where there is a U.S.G.S. gage located close enough to the put in or take out on a particular section, readings have been taken from it. Wherever possible a minimum level for solo paddling has been extablished. Generally a reading of .20 or two tenths of a foot above that listed for solo would be enough for tandem paddling. (Example: 1.54 minimum solo level; 1.74 for tandem).

On streams where a high level can be extremely dangerous a maximum reading is given whenever one has been established.

Where no U.S.G.S. gage is available gages have been painted, usually on a bridge, at a put in or take out. Generally a level of 6" below "0" can be considered a minimum for solo paddling.

Numerals—6"   Example of
Spaces—6"   6"   2   minimum water level
                      6"
                      6"   1
                      6"
                      6"   0
Surface   6"   Water Level

Gage Illustration

Whenever information can be obtained by phone, such as dam controlled streams and those entering into the Tennessee Valley, a telephone number has been given which can be called.

A recorded message giving stream flow in the Valley can be obtained on a 24-hour basis by calling (615) 525-5751. For those who like to talk to real live people and are calling from outside Tennessee, there is an (800) 251-9242 number. If calling from within the state call (800) 362-9250. Both of these lines are open 8:30-5:00 on weekdays only.

Difficulties

A brief description of specific points that might present problems for the paddler are listed, hopefully in enough detail to recognize them, but not so much as to take away the thrill of running a new river.

Directions

Detailed directions have been given to find the put in and the take out. Where there are several sections of a particuliar stream included only the put in on the first section and the take out on the last section are described. It is assumed that one who intends paddling a good bit of a river will obtain county road maps. These maps are available from the local county office of the State Highway Engineer or from:

Head of Location and Survey Unit
N.C. Department of Transportation

Division of Highways
P.O. Box 25201
Raleigh, N.C. 27611

Where a river flows through several counties reference will be made to a county route by name and number (Burke Co. Rt. 1100) initially. Thereafter only route number will be referred to until another road in the next county is introduced.

The author will appreciate any pertinent comments, corrections or suggestions which might prove valuable in any future editions.

■

Once there was a legend that told of a river that went to hear a fountain sing. The song was so beautiful that the river decided to sing it to the ocean. All the way to the shores of the ocean the river sang. Soon, the mountains heard of the song that the river was singing and came from all over the land to listen. And because the song was so beautiful the mountains settled down and stayed to listen forever.   *Algonquin Indian Legend*

Part 2
Section 1

Alarka Creek

Alarka Creek

Alarka Creek heads up in Nantahala National Forest on the slopes of the Alarka Mountains. It is a small fast stream flowing over ledges under low hanging branches. It might carry through a backyard and seconds later through inpenetrable laurel thickets that completely enclose the paddler.

On one trip a Copperhead dropped into the bow of a canoe passing downstream so the heavy foliage bears watching also. This is the only such instance the author has observed or heard of so don't let it discourage what can be a most delightful trip.

Topo Maps   Alarka, Bryson City

County   Swain

(1)   Rt. 1144 to point below Rt. 1309 bridge

Drop	Difference	Distance	Time	Scenery	Water Quality
200'	2-3	4.5 mi.	2 hrs.	A-B-C	Good

Gage   U.S.G.S. below 1309 bridge on west bank above take out and just below the old Dehart Mill. Minimum for solo run is a reading of 24.0. Can be run in later winter, spring and early summer except after an unusually dry spring.

Difficulties   The narrow passages and low overhanging branches can present problems. There are two ledges that should be scouted. They are easily recognized. A large tree blocks the passage just below old Rt. 1309 bridge. Don't be tempted to continue below the suggested take out for there is a 15' dam about 200 yds. downstream. The banks are extremely steep with no evident way to carry around. The dam cannot be seen from the road as it is located in a sharp bend directly behind the trout farm located at this point.

Directions   **Put In**—Rt. 1140 southeast off U.S. 19 west of Bryson City. Right on Rt. 1144 to creek.
Take Out—Rt. 1309 northwest off U.S. 19 (.1 mi. west of Rt. 1140) to point 200 yds. below old Rt. 1309 bridge.

Caney Fork Creek

Caney Fork Creek

The Caney Fork has its headwaters in Nantahala National Forest and is joined by many smaller rivulets as it cuts between Coward Mountain to the north and Shelton and Rich Mountains to the south and southeast. It drops over many ledges before confluencing with the Tuckaseigee River at the community of East Laport.

One may want to take a short side trip here to Judaculla Rock just north of the creek. The Rock has elaborate Indian hieroglyphics which to this time have not been interpreted. Simply follow the signs from N.C. 107.

Topo Maps   Tuckasegee, Sylva South

County   Jackson

(1)   Jackson County Rt. 1737 bridge (second bridge above N.C. 107) to 107 bridge

Drop	Difference	Distance	Time	Scenery	Water Quality
145' .8 mi. @ 50'/mi.	2	4.5 mi.	2 hrs.	A-B	Good

Gage   U.S.G.S. located alongside Rt. 1737 approximately 2.1 mi. above the put in. Minimum for solo is 3.10. Generally runnable December through the middle of May and following rains.

Difficulties   There is a cable just below the second bridge which can present problems at higher water levels. At normal levels one can easily pass under it. Also, there are a couple of ledges that drop off gradually which could present stoppers at just slightly higher water levels. This in effect would increase the run to good Class 2-3.

Directions   **Put In**—North on Rt. 1737 off N.C. 107 at the community of East Laport.
Take Out—N.C. 107 bridge at East Laport.

The run can be extended 2.1 mi. with a reading of 3.20 on the gage. Put in at the gaging station.

Cullasaja River

Cullasaja River

The Cullasaja rises in the Nantahala National Forest and drops over many falls and cascades before slowing down and entering the Little Tennessee. Three of the better known falls are Bridal Veil, Dry Falls and Cullasaja. The latter drops some 400 spectacular feet to a point about .5 mi. above the put in. U.S. 64 follows alongside the river throughout most of this area and is well worth a drive up through the gorge toward the resort village of Highlands.

Topo Maps   Scaley Mountain, Corbin Knob

County   Macon

(1)   Rt. 1678 bridge to Rt. 1668

Drop	Difference	Distance	Time	Scenery	Water Quality
120'	2-3	5.3 mi.	2.5 hrs.	B-C	Excellent to Good

Gage   U.S.G.S. on Rt. 1524 (Sugar Fork Rd.) about 40 yds. above U.S. 64 on the east bank. Minimum for solo is a reading of 2.30.

Difficulties   A fairly steep cut through a rock garden, about 150 yds. down from the put in, which is followed by a series of ledges. At higher water levels it would be best to scout this stretch.

Directions   **Put In**—Rt. 1678 (Peeks Creek Rd.) south off U.S. 64 to bridge. **Take Out**—Rt. 1668 west off U.S. 64 (just south of 64 bridge) .4 mi. to Rt. 1698.

Deep Creek

Deep Creek has its headwaters below Indian Gap (elevation 5,286') and flows through the valley between Noland Divide and Thomas Divide, which rise above it. The watershed is completely within Great Smoky Mountains National Park, thus providing it with excellent water quality. Deep Creek continues as a small, fast-moving stream with a steady gradient until just before joining the Tuckaseigee River, when it flattens out somewhat.

Tubing is one of the main forms of recreation for campers—young and old—at Deep Creek Campground, as well as for the local populace. The run is short but delightful for the experienced open boater.

Topo Map   Bryson City

County   Swain

(1)   Government road on west side of creek at gate above campground to Rt. 1340 bridge

Drop	Difference	Distance	Time	Scenery	Water Quality
66'	2	2 mi.	1 hr.	A-B	Excellent

Gage   Northwest corner of Rt. 1340 bridge. 5" below "0" is minimum for solo paddling. With a reading of 3" below "0" put in .5 mi. farther upstream, above the next bridge, for a run through a small but beautiful gorge. It can be run all year except after long dry spells.

Difficulties   Many, but none that are dangerous. At low water this requires the utmost in skill to read the small passages, to push, pull, lean and anything else to squeeze through. This is definitely not a trip for the heavy water lover. One should be on the alert for tubers during the summer.

Directions   **Put In**—Follow signs out of Bryson City to Deep Creek Campground (Rt. 1337). Continue on west side of creek to gate and put in. If gate is open proceed to first or second bridge, depending on the water level. If putting in at the second bridge, cross it and put in above 50 yds. above it. This bridge crosses Indian Creek. Deep Creek is on your left after crossing the bridge. The 1/2 mi. through the gorge drops at the rate of 50' per mi.

Take Out—Cross bridge entering into the main entrance of the campground from Rt. 1337 and turn right on Rt. 1339. Proceed approximately 2 mi. to Rt. 1340 and the take out. Ask permission at the residence behind the Baptist Church before taking out on the west bank.

Deep Creek

Hiawassee River

Hiawassee River

The Hiawassee heads up in the vicinity of Unicoi Gap in the Chattahoochee National Forest in north Georgia and runs north until the impoundment at Lake Chatuge, where it enters North Carolina. It flows generally west to the backwaters of Hiawassee Lake west of Murphy.

Topo Maps   Hayesville, Peachtree

County   Clay and Cherokee (both North Carolina)

(1)   U.S. 64 in Hayesville to Clay Co. Rt. 1302 bridge

Drop	Difficulty	Distance	Time	Scenery	Water Quality
128'	1-2	11 mi.	2.5 hrs.	A-B	Good

Gage   None. The T.V.A. Plant at Lake Chatuge is generally in operation throughout the week and under certain conditions runs on weekends. This can easily be recognizable if there are no mud flats along the river. The operation schedule is not known until after 8 p.m. the night before. Call (704) 644-5121 after that time to check for the following day.

The paddling times given on both sections are estimates for when power is being generated. When it is not add at least 2.5 hrs. to (1) and 1.5 hrs. to (2).

Difficulties   There is some fairly heavy water at shoals about .5 mi. below the mouth of Fires Creek. This spot can swamp the unwary paddler quite easily. At lower levels there are many rock and boulder gardens throughout the stretch.

(2)   Clay Co. Rt. 1302 (Shallowford) bridge to U.S. 64 west of Peachtree

Drop	Difficulty	Distance	Time	Scenery	Water Quality
137'	1-2	9.5 mi.	3 hrs.	A-B	Good

Gage   See Section (1)

Difficulties   Mission Dam, located about 1.5 mi. below the put in, should be approached cautiously. There is a log boom below sand flats on the right, which can be crossed to a fairly easy take out. Portage about 75 yds. down the old road to a well-worn path, and then another 50 yds. below the fence, to a short path to the race. The dam, operated by Alcoa, only runs when power is being generated at Lake Chatuge.

The shoals below the dam can best be scouted at this time.

Directions   **Put In**—U.S. 64 bridge in Hayesville.

Take Out—Alongside U.S. 64 2 mi. west of the American Enka Plant at Peachtree in Cherokee County.

The trip can be extended 2 mi. by taking Rt. 1140 (west of the U.S. 64 bridge) south to Rt. 1146 and putting in on the Barnard Bridge, below the dam.

Jonathans Creek

Jonathans Creek heads up at Black Camp Gap (elevation 4,522') just off the Heintooga Overlook Road from the Blue Ridge Parkway at Soco Gap. It plunges down through Maggie Valley before turning north along U.S. 276 and joining the Pigeon below I-40. It is primarily a fast run over gravel bars through farm lands above Cove Creek. Below, it changes to more of a ledge type stream cutting a small gorge as it rushes to the Pigeon.

This is a good trout stream so the paddler should be as considerate of the trout fishermen encountered along the way as possible.

Topo Map   Dellwood

County   Haywood

(1)   Haywood Co. Rt. 1394 bridge to the end of Rt. 1338 just above the confluence with the Pigeon

Drop	Difficulty	Distance	Time	Scenery	Water Quality
355'	2-3	8.8 mi.	4 hrs.	A-B-C	Good to fair

Gage   U.S.G.S. located on Rt. 1338 approximately .5 mi. above the confluence with the Pigeon. Minimum reading for solo is 1.50.

Difficulties   About 1 mi. below the put in there is a chute on the right blocked off by an overhanging tree limb. This is recognizable by a small channel running to the left toward a large silo. This can be carried or lined easily on the small island there.

In the area down from the 276 bridge there is a ledge which presents a fair sized hydraulic at levels above 2.00. This is about .25 mi. below a broken foot bridge and at higher levels should be scouted. Approximately .4 mi. below the I-40 bridge there is a series of ledges where a drop of about 15' occurs within some 100 yds. There is an old automobile in the creek, which marks the beginning of this run. The entire stretch can be easily scouted on the left bank.

Directions   **Put In**—North on U.S. 276 off U.S. 19 at Dellwood for approximately .5 mi., to the Rt. 1394 bridge on the left. The creek runs beside 276 at this point.

Take Out—North on U.S. 276 to the second bridge across the creek (south of I-40). Go left along the south side of the creek and cross the Rt. 1338 bridge across Cove Creek. Follow Rt. 1338 along Jonathans Creek to its end, and take out about 100 yds. above the old house at the end of the road.

Note: At a water level of 2.50 on the gage a run of about 3 mi., from the Rt. 1306 bridge (off U.S. 19) to the second bridge of Rt. 1307 can be made. However, about .25 mi. of posted property is just downstream from this take out so a run on down to the put in point on Rt. 1394 might present problems. This 3 mi. stretch is quite fast and narrow with a gradient averaging almost 75' per mi.

■

I am glad I shall never be young without wild country to be young in. Of what avail are forty freedoms without a blank spot on the map?

Aldo Leopold

Little Tennessee River

Little Tennessee River

The Little Tennessee first appears to the traveler on U.S. 23-441 south of Franklin as a small creek. One will wonder how such a small stream can grow to a full size river between there and Iotla. It flows generally north between the Nantahala Mountain Range on the west and the Cowee Range to the east before reaching the impoundment at Fontana.

The riverside alternates between farmlands and woodlands in section 1, while below Lost Bridge it becomes heavily forested, except where Rt. 1114 hits it occasionally. The area near Franklin and around much of Macon Co. is widely known for its great mineral deposits and is certainly a rock hound's heaven.

The "Little T" is one of the few rivers in North Carolina that lend themselves to overnight canoe camping. Generally speaking there is enough water to carry gear and at the same time the rapids aren't so formidable that the paddler is likely to finish the day with it wet. Unfortunately there aren't many streams remaining that can claim both these qualities. The good ones have either been "dammed" leaving nothing but flat water, are too shallow to carry the necessary equipment, or are too rough to maneuver through rapids with the extra weight in the boat.

Topo Maps   Franklin, Alarka, Wesser

Counties   Macon and Swain

(1)   N.C. 28 bridge at Iotla to Lost Bridge

Drop	Difficulty	Distance	Time	Scenery	Water Quality
50'	1-2	10 mi.	4.5 hrs.	A-B	Good

Gage   U.S.G.S. gage on left bank .8 mi. north of Needmore and approximately 6.8 mi. below Lost Bridge Road bridge. The "Little T" is very seldom too low to run. Only following extreme dry periods would it be so low.

Difficulties   None. The first several miles are flat with an occasional riffle. There are a few shallow ledges in the latter part of the section.

(2) Lost Bridge, off N.C. 28, to U.S. 19 bridge

Drop	Difficulty	Distance	Time	Scenery	Water Quality
182'	2-3/4	13 mi.	4.5 hrs.	A	Good

Gage   See section (1). The lower section can become dangerous with high water levels when Lake Fontana is low. To check on the streamflow call (615) 637-0101, Ext. 2054. Minimum reading is about 350 c.f.s., while the maximum will be approximately 2000 c.f.s.

Difficulties   There are several ledges which should be approached cautiously in higher levels.

When Fontana is quite low there is a series of ledges which run for close to 250 yds. At the end of this rapid the entire river, which previously has been up to 300 ft. wide, narrows down to rush through an area no wider than 20 ft. Before Fontana Dam innundated the river, this part was known as "The Narrows."

"The Narrows" should definitely be scouted before attempting to run. In higher waters the entire rapid can be quite formidable and should be scouted. The standing wave created at the bottom of "The Narrows" is as high as 5 ft. at higher levels. At lower levels scout on the left; at higher levels, scout on the right.

The water level of Lake Fontana is generally lowered during the winter in preparation for the spring rains.

Directions   **Put In**—N.C. 28 bridge at Iotla, about 4 mi. north of Franklin.
Take Out—U.S. 19-N.C. 28 bridge southwest of Bryson City.
Paddle beyond the bridge to the right bank, to a small "goat path" which cuts back up under the bridge. This isn't recommended for potential coronary victims. Even if one doesn't fall into this class, there may be some question before reaching the top when the lake is low.

Nantahala River

Nantahala River

The Nantahala heads up in the edge of Nantahala National Forest before entering Aquone Lake, reportedly the highest lake in North Carolina. From there it is piped and tunneled down the mountain to the power plant a few yards above the put in point. The water enters the river at a temperature averaging around 45°F. The river then flows down through the beautiful Nantahala Gorge in a mad shivering dash to Lake Fontana. Nantahala, meaning "Land-of-the-noon-day-sun," was the name given by the Cherokee Indians, because of the deep gorge which shuts out the sun for most of each day.

The cold water can create an unusual phenomenon on a very warm day. A fog rises about 3 ft. above the water, sometimes cutting visibility down to a few feet. Such visibility doesn't leave the newcomer to the river with much margin for error.

After one has had some of the icy water splashed into the boat, it is a rather chilling experience to observe some hardy young souls tubing down the river. This has to be where the "Dead End Kids" got their start.

The course begins at Patton's Pool and runs to the take out, below Nantahala Falls, with continuous white water. A bailer—make that a *big* bailer—is a necessity for the canoeist running the Nantahala. The constant action makes this the most popular canoeing river in the state.

Nantahala Outdoor Center, located at Wesser, below Nantahala Falls, is operated by Payson and Aurelia Kennedy. They conduct guided canoe and raft trips down the river beginning in the spring and continuing on into the fall. This is an excellent way for the uninitiated to try the river for the first time. N.O.C. also has a small restaurant, a store, and motel accommodations. For those who wish to camp, Lost Mine Campground, which is privately owned, is located on Swain Co. Rt. 1103 only one mile from Wesser.

Topo Maps   Hewitt, Wesser

Counties   Macon and Swain

(1)   Power Plant to Wesser

Drop	Difficulty	Distance	Time	Scenery	Water Quality
265'	3/4	8 mi.	2.5 hrs.	A-B	Excellent

Gage   The river can be run only when the power plant is operating, which is generally the case during the week, and quite frequently on weekends. Phone (615) 525-5721 to determine whether or not the plant is in operation (also refer to section titled "Explanation").

Difficulties   Below the put in at the forks, Patton's Run begins. It is a long Class 3, requiring the paddler to stay to the inside of the bend. This is heavy fast water. It, as well as most of the river, can be scouted from U.S. 19, which follows the river very closely throughout the run. Scout this one from the pull off on the highway, before launching.

Patton's Pool and Run were dedicated to Charlie Patton of Brevard, N.C., an avid paddler of the Nantahala despite the fact that he had practically no use of one arm. He passed on later in the day following a trip down his beloved river.

The river continues along its fast course with little letup for the next 7.5 mi.

Nantahala Falls, which is about 400 yds. above Nantahala Outdoor Center, is a Class 4, which at higher levels easily becomes a Class 5. There is a short quiet pool above it where one can pull over easily—either to scout the falls or to pull out. It is a small section of flat land on the right with a well marked path. The entrance and approach to the falls is rather difficult and can put a lot of water in the boat before one hits the falls. Be sure to empty the boat before attempting to run. The entrance is generally where the novice or low intermediate skilled paddler gets in trouble, only to be finished off in the falls.

The falls consist of two ledges. The top one doesn't extend all the way across the river, and the passage is just on the left end of it. The paddler then must cut hard back to the right to catch the tongue on the lower drop. With higher water the upper ledge can be run straight through on the right, therefore lining up for the tongue below. This is about 3 ft. off the large boulder on the right.

In the event one swamps or dumps in the falls, get control of the craft immediately. Wesser Falls, which is .25 mi. downstream, will only spew out little pieces.

Directions   **Put In**—North on U.S. 19 from Wesser and N.O.C. to the first paved road on the left (Macon Co. Rt. 1310). Cross the small bridge, and the put in is in the clearing on the left at the forks.

Take Out—Along U.S. 19 between Nantahala Falls and Wesser.

Oconaluftee River

The Oconaluftee heads up between Indian Gap (elevation 5,286') and Newfound Gap (elevation 5,048') and generally flows beside U.S. 441 through the Great Smoky Mountains National Park, until it confluences with the Tuckaseigee River east of Bryson City. The run above Cherokee is one through many rock gardens in crystal clear water. Below Cherokee the water quality diminishes considerably due to sewage being dumped in. A distinct odor may be noticeable below the 441 bridge, but it doesn't continue for long.

The river enters the Cherokee Indian Reservation .5 mi. below its confluence with the Raven's Fork River, and from this point to the take out is designated as "Enterprise Waters." This stretch can be paddled only on Tuesdays during trout season, when the river is being stocked (first Saturday in April to the last of October).

The approximately 4.5 mi. stretch above the reservation boundary can be paddled at any time. In order to do so one should check in at the ranger station at Park Headquarters, which is located at Pioneer Structures on U.S. 441 north of Cherokee, to inform them of plans to canoe the river. This might save one from being "pulled" off the river by park rangers. This actually happened to Ed Gertler several years ago. It could not only prove embarrassing, but could also lead to a rather long hike.

Topo Maps   Smokemont, Whittier

County   Swain

(1)   Smokemont Campground to Birdtown

Drop	Difficulty	Distance	Time	Scenery	Water Quality
308'	2.3	11.5 mi.	4.5 hrs.	A-B-C	Excellent to Poor

Gage   U.S.G.S. gage is on the south bank 200 ft. upstream from the Rt. 1359 bridge below Birdtown. Minimum for solo run is 1.70. It can be run at 1.32 from Ravensford Bridge (above Pioneer Structures), which cuts about 4. mi. off the total trip. A gage directly across on the opposite bank (along U.S. 19) will read approximately .05 lower than the opposite gage, so estimate accordingly.

Difficulties   There are many tight runs over ledges and through gravel bars that require fast thinking and faster maneuvering.

After entering Cherokee, there are the remains of an old washed-out dam along 441. Iron rods protrude from some of the rocks and it is best to run on the far right directly behind the trailer. This is located about 80 yds. above the Cherokee Information Station and picnic area.

For anyone wishing to extend the trip into the Tuckaseigee, or on to Bryson City, there is a 30 ft. dam 3 mi. below Birdtown. It can be portaged on the right.

Directions   **Put In**—U.S. 441 north of Cherokee, towards Gatlinburg, Tenn. to the entrance to Smokemont Campground; cross bridge.
                      Take Out—U.S. 19 west of Cherokee to Birdtown; cross the Rt. 1359 bridge (at Cherokee Recreation Park Campground sign),
to the gage.

Oconaluftee River

Pigeon River

The Pigeon meanders through farm land above Canton. In Canton it becomes rather polluted, primarily due to Champion International, which has made some progress in cleaning up the river, but there is still a long way to go. Several miles below Canton the river flows through a deep gorge with I-40 running high above it. The "Dry Gorge," between Waterville Lake and the Walters Plant, is just that, except in periods of extremely high water when expert decked boaters possibly could run it. The distance is approximately 13 mi.

The river below Walters Plant becomes a natural slalom run through a rock strewn course. This could be made into one of the finest slalom courses in the east, but for the amount of pollution.

Topo Maps   Waynesville, Cruso, Canton, Clyde, Fines Creek; Waterville, Hartford, and Newport (Tenn.)

Counties   Haywood (N.C.); Cocke (Tenn.)

(1)   Confluence of East and West Forks of the Pigeon to U.S. 19-23 bridge

Drop	Difficulty	Distance	Time	Scenery	Water Quality
58'	1-2	5 mi.	2 hrs.	B	Fair

Gage   On west side of N.C. 110 bridge at the put in. Minimum for solo 6" below "0." The river can be run from here down most of the year, except during long dry spells.

Difficulties   None.

(2)   U.S. 19-23 bridge in Canton to Ferguson bridge

Drop	Difficulty	Distance	Time	Scenery	Water Quality
158'	1-2	15.6 mi.	6.5 hrs.	B-C	Poor

Gage   Minimum level for solo: 7" below "0."

Difficulties   None. Primarily, the difficulty will be with the olfactory nerves.

(3) Ferguson Bridge (Haywood Co. Rts. 1355 and 1363) to New Hepco Bridge

Drop	Difficulty	Distance	Time	Scenery	Water Quality
157'	2-3/4-5	6.1 mi.	2.5 hrs.	B	Poor

Gage   Minimum level for solo: 7" below "0."

Difficulties   There is a boulder garden which drops 8 ft. in 20 yds., with standing waves at the bottom (Class 4). This can be recognized by a long stretch of flat water after having paddled along I-40 for some distance. A short rapid just above tends to lead one into the fast water before one recognises the danger. Passage at a normal water level is through the second chute from the right. Scout on the right.

A second long flat stretch precedes the Class 5, which is 600 yds. above the take out. An old dam 4 ft. high, with a heavy hydraulic, is followed by 60 yds. of rather heavy water. The paddler must move from far right to far left through here if attempting to run the dam, or even below it. This hydraulic held a C-1 paddler in for a few anxious moments before he got out. However, his boat remained tumbling for some 30 minutes before a tandem team was able to hook a grab loop and pull it out. One break in the old wall may be run on the far right. *Do not* attempt to run straight down on the right all the way. Cut to the left above the large rock at the bottom of the run.

(4) Below the Walters Plant of Carolina Power and Light to the bridge at Hartford, Tenn.

Drop	Difficulty	Distance	Time	Scenery	Water Quality
78'	3-4	4.5 mi.	2.5 hrs.	A-B	Poor

Gage   None. Call (704) 486-5965 and ask for the water flow from Walters Plant. It is generally in operation. A reading of 50,000 k.w. is maximum for solo open boats.

Difficulties   There are several rapids that should be scouted. Most of these can be seen from the road or highway. The water volume is generally large and presents many large standing waves and souseholes to give any but the most advanced paddlers trouble galore. At a run of 50,000 k.w. one has all the water he'll care to see from an open boat.

Pigeon River

(5)   Bridge at Hartford (Tenn.) to Cocke Co. Rt 2484 bridge

Drop	Difficulty	Distance	Time	Scenery	Water Quality
125'	1-2+	8 mi.	3.5 hrs.	A-B-C	Poor

Gage   None. Runnable most of the year, except during dry spells.

Difficulties None. There are many ledges on the section between the two
                  I-40 bridges. At higher water levels this stretch can be fairly tur-
bulent.

Directions   **Put In**—N.C. 110 and Haywood Co. 1105 at the confluence
                  of the East and West Forks, south of Canton.
                  Take Out—Section 3. New Hepco bridge off I-40 at Fines Creek
                  Exit, north of Canton.
                  Section 5. Take I-40 exit 440 and go west to the first right; pro-
                  ceed to Rt. 2484 bridge. An easier takeout may be made along
the road on the west side of the river .25 mi. above the bridge.

For those who might like to extend the trip, a run of 7.5 mi. to U.S. 25-70
bridge north of Newport (Tenn.) (an easy take out) can be made. This stretch
is fairly flat, but has enough riffles scattered along the way to be interesting,
plus some good scenery.

Pigeon River, East Fork

The East Fork of the Pigeon is a shallow low water stream meandering through farm land as it courses back and forth under U.S. 276 before finally joining the West Fork.

Topo Map   Cruso

County   Haywood

(1)   Rt. 1887 bridge (Pisgah Creek Rd.) to N.C. 110 bridge

Drop	Difficulty	Distance	Time	Scenery	Water Quality
258'	2-3	8.7 mi.	4 hrs.	B	Good

Gage   On northwest side of N.C. 110 bridge. Minimum for solo: 6" below "0." You must go down to water level in order to read the gage. Generally runnable during wet seasons, or early spring.

Difficulties   None. The river has a fairly constant gradient with no abrupt drops. At one point the river flows through a gravel pit, which gets rather shallow. This area is evident from the highway. There are 2 or 3 posted signs through this area, which primarily refer to fishing.

Directions   **Put In**—Rt. 1887 bridge east from U.S. 176 (at the community of Caruso), and southeast of the intersection of U.S. 276 and NC. 110.
Take Out—N.C. 110 bridge, 1 mi. north of intersection of U.S. 276 and N.C. 110, at the confluence with the West Fork.

Pigeon River, East Fork   Pigeon River, West Fork

Pigeon River, West Fork

The West Fork of the Pigeon heads up in the Pisgah National Forest, then flows through Champion Papers' property at Lake Logan before confluencing with the East Fork. The put in is about .25 mi. below the dam at Lake Logan. From there down it is a fast moving low water stream flowing over a series of gravel beds.

Topo Map   Waynesville

County   Haywood

(1) Junction of Rt. N.C. 215 and Rt. 1129 to confluence with East Fork of the Pigeon

Drop	Difficulty	Distance	Time	Scenery	Water Quality
204'	2-3	6.3 mi.	2 hrs.	B	Excellent to Good

Gage   U.S.G.S. gage is on the east bank, downstream at the Rt. 1111 bridge. Minimum for solo: 1.80. Generally runnable during wet seasons, or early spring.

Difficulties   There are several fast runs through long gravel bars. In addition to these, there is one hard "S" turn dropping over two ledges, which is located just beyond a high undercut clay bank as the river bears to the left.

Directions   **Put In**—N.C. 215 bridge at the junction of 215 and 1129 (Little East Fork Rd.), below Champion Papers, Inc. property line. Rt. 1111 is a continuation of N.C. 110, after crossing U.S. 276.

Take Out—N.C. 110 bridge, 1 mi. north of the intersection of U.S. 276 and N.C. 110, at the confluence with the East Fork.

Raven Fork River

The Raven Fork comes off Breakneck Ridge at what quite often seems to be at just that speed. It flows through the Cherokee Indian Reservation to a point just above the town of Cherokee, where it joins the Oconaluftee River.

It runs through boulder fields and rock gardens, to present one of the most delightful trips the paddler can find anywhere. The Cherokee have designated the river as "Enterprise Waters," (see Oconaluftee), thereby closing the main stretch to paddling, except on Wednesdays. The short stretch running from the National Park Boundary, just above "Crack-in-the-Rock" down to the confluence, is runnable on Tuesdays only, as is the Oconaluftee. At this time there is a possibility that a "winter" or extended trout season may be established by the Indians. Therefore, one may want to check at the Police Station in Cherokee to find out the status of the river before putting in during the normal "off season."

Topo Maps   Bunches Bald, Smokemont

County   Swain

(1)   Confluence with the Straight Fork to the bridge at the Job Corps Center

Drop	Difficulty	Distance	Time	Scenery	Water Quality
408'	3-4	8 mi.	4 hrs.	A-B	Excellent
1@60'/mi.					
1/2@ 75'/mi.					

Gage   U.S.G.S. gage is at Sherrills Cove bridge. Minimum for solo: 1.50. Maximum for a safe run through the gorge: 2.50. At a level of 1.50 it would be best to cut the trip shorter and put in at the confluence of Bunches Creek.

Difficulties   There is a rapid with a large hydraulic just below the put in which may encourage one to start below it. It makes for a rather unpleasant trip to take two strokes and find oneself out of the boat. The river drops at a rate of 75'/mi. through the first .5 mi. Fortunately this stretch, as well as much of the rest of the trip, can be scouted from the road, and it will be wise to do so through here.

There are numerous Class 3 rapids before reaching the first Class 4 , which cannot be seen completely from the road. This rapid is in the bend of the river behind Smith Memorial Pentecostal Holiness Church. With a higher water level it requires a great deal of difficult maneuvering to prevent swamping the canoe.

After passing Sherrills Cove Creek bridge the river enters a 900 ft. deep gorge and makes a large bend around River Valley Camp, a private campground. There are three Class 4's in the gorge, all of which should be scouted. The gradient increases to over 60'/mi. The approach to the first two rapids will vary somewhat with the water level, but both can be scouted from the right. The third, "Crack-in-the-Rock," can be scouted on the left and run on the left. It is located just beyond the campground and just above the National Park boundary sign. There is fairly heavy water above the rapid, so care should be taken in the approach.

Directions   **Put In**—Take the Government Road east of the U.S. 441 bridge over the Oconaluftee in Cherokee for approximately 10 mi. **Take Out**—Turn west on the first paved road south of Government Road bridge crossing the Raven Fork. This road goes into the Job Corps Center. Take out can be made at this bridge or at the first one (Government Rd.) for a slightly shorter run.

Raven Fork River

Soco Creek

Soco Creek heads up in Soco Gap (elevation 4,345′), where the Blue Ridge Parkway crosses U.S. 19, east of Cherokee at the Qualla Reservation line. It flows to its confluence with the Oconaluftee River just below the take out. It presents the skilled paddler with a real roller-coaster ride. Although it never strays more than a few yards from U.S. 19, and runs through many backyards, one has little opportunity to view the scenery—good or bad.

Soco is wholly within the reservation and has been designated as "Enterprise Waters." This means that it is open to trout fishermen and is stocked by the tribe. For this reason it can be run only on Tuesdays during trout season, when it is being stocked. At this time, the possibility exists that an extended or "winter" trout season may be established by the Indians. For this reason it might be best to check at the Police Station in Cherokee to learn the status of the stream before putting in during the normal "off season."

Topo Maps   Sylva North, Whittier

County   Jackson

(1)   Soco Creek Rd. and U.S. 19 to U.S. 441 bridge

Drop	Difficulty	Distance	Time	Scenery	Water Quality
566′	2-3-4	8.5 mi.	3 hrs.	B	Excellent
1-3/5 mi. @ 106′/mi.					

Gage   U.S. 19 bridge on the southwest side, across from El Camino Restaurant. A reading of 6″ below "0" is minimum for a run from U.S. 19 bridge, while a reading of 2″ below "0" will allow a run from the first put in. Dredging is still being done in some stretches, which will possibly affect the level through those areas.

Difficulties   This is a natural slalom course with no big drops, but several rapids might require scouting, especially in the upper 1.75 mi. which drops at the rate of 106′/mi. Much of the run can be scouted from the highway. Below Bluewing Rd. the channel is being changed some due to dredging. Stay to the left here, although this may get into a rather shallow stretch due to rechannelization.

Directions   **Put In**—Soco Creek Rd. where it leaves U.S. 19, going up the creek across from Soco Trail Campground.
Take Out—U.S. 441 bridge, 1 mi. south of Cherokee.

Tuckaseigee River

Tuckaseigee River

The Tuckaseigee begins in the Nantahala National Forest, where the East Fork and the West Fork of the Tuckaseigee confluence. (For information on each of the forks, see directions for the put in.) From there it meanders through a valley with a highway following along its entire length, except for about 4 mi. It flows through Bryson City before entering Lake Fontana.

The river primarily runs over gravel bars until it reaches the gorge below Dillsboro, where it begins to drop over ledges. After leaving the gorge it resumes its original characteristics, with a few ledges and shoals interspersed.

The water quality down from Dillsboro was very poor due to industrial pollution prior to late 1974, when the culprit responsible for it closed down. Since that time the river has steadily improved.

Topo Maps   Tuckasegee, Sylva South, Green's Creek, Whittier, Bryson City

Counties   Jackson, Swain

(1)   N.C. 107 bridge at the community of Tuckaseigee to dam at Cullowhee

Drop	Difficulty	Distance	Time	Scenery	Water Quality
84'	1-2/3	9.5 mi.	3 hrs.	B	Good

Gage   U.S.G.S. gage is on the left bank at the foot of River St. in Bryson City, or about 150 yds. below the old bridge in the center of town. No reading is available for a minimum level. Generally the river can be run year 'round except during extremely dry spells. A better run is likely if the power plants on the East Fork and West Fork are in operation (see Directions).

Difficulties   There is a low Class 3 rapid beyond East Laport, where the river bends away from the highway. It runs continuously for over 100 yds. Approach it in the center.

The take out at Cullowhee is above a 10 ft. dam. It should be approached cautiously. Take out or carry on the right side.

(2)   Dam at Cullowhee to dam at Dillsboro

Drop	Difficulty	Distance	Time	Scenery	Water Quality
88'	1-2	11 mi.	4.5 hrs.	B	Good

Tuckaseigee River

Gage   See section (1).

Difficulties   Small riffles and gravel bars, primarily. The take out at Dillsboro
              is above a 15 ft. dam. An easy take out can be made about 50
yds. above the dam on the right.
    For those who wish to continue the trip into section (3), take out should be
made on the left in the flats, about 75 yds. above the dam. This will require a
portage of about 250 yds. to the road and back down a steep path to a sandy
beach below the dam.

(3)   Dam at Dillsboro to Rt. 1392 bridge

Drop	Difficulty	Distance	Time	Scenery	Water Quality
74'	2-3	5 mi.	1.5 hrs.	A-B-C	Poor

Gage   See section (1).

Difficulties   The river drops through a steep gorge while running through
              rock gardens and over ledges, several of which may require
scouting.

(4)   Rt. 1392 bridge at Barkers Creek to the intersection of Shoal Creek Rd. and U.S. 19, west of Whittier

Drop	Difficulty	Distance	Time	Scenery	Water Quality
58'	1-2	8 mi.	3 hrs.	B	Poor

Gage   Can be run all year.

Difficulties   None.

(5)   Intersection of Shoal Creek Rd. and U.S. 19 west of Whittier to Bryson City

Drop	Difficulty	Distance	Time	Scenery	Water Quality
108'	2-3/4	8 mi.	3.5 hrs.	B	Poor

Gage   Runnable all year except during extremely dry periods. A read-
              ing of 3.75 on the Bryson City gage would be suggested maxi-

mum level for intermediate paddlers. At this level some of the shoals can get quite heavy.

Difficulties   Shortly after leaving the put in, the river runs through an area of shoals which at medium high water can kick up some pretty good waves. This can be best run by staying to the right most of the way. Also, it will keep the paddler from being swept over a double ledge at the bottom, a low Class 4. It can be recognized by the first short flat stretch as the river bends right, below the longest continuous shoals. The river drops about 7 ft. in 15 yds. It can be run in several different ways, depending on the water level. Scout from the right bank.

Just after passing under the railroad bridge below Ela, there is a rapid on the right which will have a large hydraulic in medium high water levels.

A series of shoals begin just above the U.S. 19 bridge in Bryson City. These should be approached carefully.

The last rapid above the take out consists of a long run down the left, and ends in a right angle turn. This is known as "Devil's Dip." The right turn should be made soon enough to miss the rather nice souse hole that waits to gobble up the paddler who lets his canoe drift too far to the outside of the turn.

Directions   **Put In**—N.C. 107 bridge, southeast of Cullowhee, at the community of Tuckaseigee.

The trip can be extended 1.5 mi. by putting in on the West Fork, when the Thorpe Power Plant is operating. The put in is found by driving up N.C. 107 along the West Fork, to where the water enters the streambed. This is a very narrow run down very fast water.

If the Main Plant is operating on the East Fork, the run can be extended about 2 mi. by driving up Rt. 1135 to River Park Campground, which is located immediately below the dam on Lake Cedar Cliff.

Information on whether the Main Plant is operating can be obtained by calling Nantahala Power in Sylva, (704) 293-5137.

Take Out—On the left bank downstream from the first bridge in Bryson City. Go north on the road to Deep Creek Campground off Main St. (U.S. 19), and take a left into the parking lot. On Sunday an automobile can be left here, but on weekdays try the Federal Building parking lot, which is west on Main St.

Tuckaseigee River

Tusquitee Creek

Tusquitee Creek

Tusquitee Creek heads up in Nantahala National Forest and runs along south of the Tusquitee Mountains. It flows primarily through a pastoral region before confluencing with the Hiawassee downstream from Hayesville.

Topo Maps   Shooting Creek, Hayesville

County   Clay

(1)   Rt. 1330 bridge to Rt. 1300 bridge

Drop	Difficulty	Distance	Time	Scenery	Water Quality
140'	1-2	5.2 mi.	2.5 hrs.	A-B	Good

Gage   On the southwest side of R. 1307 bridge at the junction of Rt. 1326. Minimum level for solo: 5" below the bottom of "0." Can be run most all year except during dry spells.

Difficulties   None. Primarily a series of small rock gardens interspersed with an occasional ledge; however, be on the lookout for downed trees blocking the passage.

Directions   **Put In**—Take Tusquitee St. north out of Hayesville across the Hiawassee and bear northeast on Rt. 1307 to the gage. Go beyond it approximately 3.5 mi. to Rt. 1330 and south to the bridge.
Take Out—Take Tusquitee St. across the Hiawassee and bear northwest on Rt. 1300 approximately 1 mi. to the take out bridge.
The trip can be extended 2.5 mi. by continuing on to the Hiawassee and downstream on it to the second bend, coming close to Rt. 1300. Take out at the junction of Rt. 1345 with Rt. 1300.

Section 2

Big Laurel Creek

This is a fast wild water stream cutting a gorge 1,200 ft. deep between Mill Ridge on the north and Walnut Knob on the south. This is truly a most spectacular scenic run. Unfortunately, as with many trips of this type, one isn't able to raise his eyes from the job at hand long enough to be able to enjoy nature's wonders to the fullest.

Big Laurel flows into the French Broad 3.5 mi. above Hot Springs. This section must be run unless the paddler goes upstream 1/4 mi. to the community of Stackhouse (see the French Broad River, section (9)).

Topo Maps   White Rock, Hot Springs

County   Madison

(1)   U.S.25 and 70 bridge to 25-70 bridge over the French Broad in Hot Springs

Drop	Difficulty	Distance	Time	Scenery	Water Quality
200'	3-4	4 mi.	3 hrs.	AA	Good
.5 mi.@80'/mi.					

Gage   At Rt. 25-70 bridge on the east side. Reading of 6" below "0" is minimum for solo run. At this level two rapids must be carried. A reading of 3" above the bottom of "0" is the maximum level recommended. The great increase in difficulty with the slight increase in level is due to the constricted course. It can be run except in extremely dry seasons.

Difficulties   There are many rapids that should be scouted, the first of which is .25 mi. below the put in. An innocuous looking 2 ft. ledge which is run on the left pushes the bow squarely into a pointed rock at the bottom of the chute. This ledge can be recognized by the cottage just below it on the left bank, which is the last sign of habitation until the railroad bridge 100 yds. above the confluence with the French Broad. This ledge is a warning of bigger and better things to come.

Some other rapids worth mentioning are: The "Stair Steps," a tightly constricted series 3 drops of 3 ft. each, which becomes quite hairy at even 2" below "0" gage. "Suddy Hole," an 8 ft. ledge which can be run on the left at water levels above the bottom of "0," and on the right by those with suicidal tendencies. The "Narrows," easily recognized, certainly should be scouted to determine the best passage. The bed of an old railroad runs on the south side the entire length of the creek, which can help one in scouting.

The previously mentioned railroad bridge marks the end of the Big Laurel run and the beginning of big water on the French Broad (see section (9) of the French Broad River).

Directions   **Put In**—On the east side of U.S. 25-70 bridge over the Big Laurel.

Take Out—West side beneath the U.S. 25-70 bridge.

Big Laurel Creek

Broad River

The Broad drops through beautiful Hickory Nut Gorge, then flows through boulder gardens as it courses by the towns of Bat Cave and Chimney Rock before entering the impoundment at Lake Lure. It is below Lake Lure that the paddler can pick up the fast moving water to cruise on. Most of the rapids on this section are found between the dam and the first river bridge at Uree. Beyond Uree the Broad follows U.S. 64-74 closely for some 2.5 mi. before cutting away through a heavily wooded and rather remote area to the take out. For those who might want to continue farther down the Broad (some additional 113 mi.), see 6.1.

Topo Map   Lake Lure

County   Rutherford

(1)   Dam at Lake Lure to Rutherford Co. Rt. 1181

Drop	Difficulty	Distance	Time	Scenery	Water Quality
89'	1-2	7.4 mi.	2.75 hrs.	A-B	Good

Gage   On U.S. 64-74 bridge at Uree, on southeast pillar. Reading of 6'' below "0" minimum for solo run. The entire section can only be run when water is coming through the dam.

Difficulties   When the water is coming through the dam, the section between the dam and the bridge at Uree can be run, otherwise the water level will be too low. There are several ledges through here that require some fast maneuvering. Another short set of ledges are located beyond the confluence of Cove Creek. Watch for logs blocking the passages below Uree bridge, wher the river splits into several channels.

Directions   **Put In**—North off U.S. 64-74 1 mi. east of the bridge at Uree to dam. You must carry the boat down steps on south end of the dam.
Take Out—Go 6.8 mi. east on U.S. 64-74 from the bridge at Uree to Rt. 1181, then south to the Rt. 1181 bridge.

Broad River

Davidson River

The Davidson heads up in the Nantahala National Forest. Although U.S. 276 is never over 100 yds. away from the river, the paddler is hardly aware of the fact while floating through the scenic setting. The gradient is very gradual as it flows over gravel bars and small ledges. An outstanding point of interest in the area is Looking Glass Mountain, a large granite dome, which presents many challenging routes for the rock climber.

Topo Maps   Shining Rock, Pisgah Forest

County   Transylvania

(1)   Confluence of Davidson and Lookingglass Creek to U.S. 276 bridge

Drop	Difficulty	Distance	Time	Scenery	Water Quality
132'	1-2	6.1 mi.	2 hrs.	A	Excellent

Gage   U.S.G.S. gage is located 50 yds. above the 276-64 bridge, on the west bank. Minimum reading for solo run is 1.0.

Difficulties   None. Primarily small ledges and gravel bars. With a reading of 1.4 a slightly longer and more exciting run can be made by driving 1.4 mi. farther up the forest road and putting in at the Fish Hatchery. Total gradient on this stretch is approximately 60 ft.

Directions   **Put In**—Northwest of Brevard on U.S. 276 to Lookingglass Creek bridge. Pull off to the left on the forest road.
Take Out—U.S. 276-64 bridge northeast of Brevard.

Davidson River

First Broad River

The First Broad rises on the slopes of South Mountain and flows easterly through Golden Valley below the South Mountain range before cutting south through central Cleveland County and joining the Broad River below Shelby.

The upper stretches meander through the foothills, many of which are filled with mountain laurel and rhododendron.

Topo Maps   Benn Knob, Shelby

Counties   Rutherford, Cleveland

(1)   Rutherford Co. Rt. 1726 bridge to Rt. 1737 bridge.

Drop	Difficulty	Distance	Time	Scenery	Water Quality
114'	1-2	8.8 mi.	3 hrs.	A	Good

Gage   U.S.G.S. gage is located 75 yds. above Cleveland Co. Rt. 1530 bridge on the south bank. Minimum level for solo run is 1.52.

Difficulties   None. Primarily pebble fields with occasional ledges. The stretch below Rt. 1734, which is filled with laurel and rhododendron, is particularly scenic.

(2)   Rutherford Co. Rt. 1737 bridge to Cleveland Co. Rt. 1529 bridge

Drop	Difficulty	Distance	Time	Scenery	Water Quality
64'	1-2	6.1 mi.	2.5 hrs.	A-B	Good

Gage   U.S.G.S. minimum is 1.47.

Difficulties   None, other than many small pebble fields. The lower half of the run has many trees down, presenting a natural slalom for the paddler.

Directions   **Put In**—Southeast on N.C. 226 from U.S. 64 to Rutherford Rt. 1726 (50 yds. west of the river bridge), then southwest for 1.1. mi. to the put in bridge.

Take Out—N.C. 226 south of the Rutherford-Cleveland Co. line to Cleveland Rt. 1529, then northeast .5 mi. to the take out bridge.

First Broad River

French Broad

The French Broad is formed in the vicinity of Rosman, N.C., where the North Fork, West Fork, Middle Fork, and East Fork join together. The upper reaches of the river are primarily flat, flowing over shallow shoals alternating between farm lands and wooded areas. It is ideal for quiet float trips.

From Asheville down to Hot Springs the river cuts through a more mountainous area and changes complexion greatly as the volume and gradient increase. It becomes a wide powerful force, flowing through scenic gorges, over series of ledges, and through large boulders. The river here requires a much higher level of skill from the paddler.

Below Hot Springs the river slows down to flat stretches interspersed with rapids, along with some outstanding rock formations, such as Paint Rock and Chimney Rock.

Topo Maps   Rosman, Brevard, Pisgah Forest, Horseshoe, Skyland, Asheville, Weaverville, Leicester, Marshall, Spring Creek, Hot Springs (N.C.); Paint Rock and Needy Mountain (Tenn.)

Counties   Transylvania, Henderson, Buncombe, Madison (N.C.); Cocke (Tenn.)

(1)   U.S. 64 bridge over the North Fork west of Rosman to Transylvania Rt. 1110 bridge

Drop	Difficulty	Distance	Time	Scenery	Water Quality
54'	1-2	10.5 mi.	4.5 hrs.	A-B-C	Good

Gage   None. The river is runnable all year, except during periods of extreme dryness and even then the lower section can be run. See section (9) for maximum safe level.

Difficulties   None. Primarily flat running over shallows and shoals.

(2)   Transylvania Rt. 1110 bridge (Island Ford Road) to U.S. 276 bridge

Drop	Difficulty	Distance	Time	Scenery	Water Quality
34'	1	10.3 mi.	4 hrs.	A-B-C	Good

Difficulties   None. Same as (1).

(3)   U.S. 276 bridge south of Brevard to U.S. 64 bridge

Drop	Difficulty	Distance	Time	Scenery	Water Quality
41'	1	21 mi.	8.5 hrs.	A-B-C	Fair

Difficulties   None. Same as (1).

(4)   U.S. 64 bridge west of Henderson in Henderson Co. to N.C. 280 bridge

Drop	Difficulty	Distance	Time	Scenery	Water Quality
37'	1	17 mi.	7 hrs.	A-B	Fair

Difficulties   None. Same as (1).

(5)   N.C. 280 bridge (Long Shoals bridge) in Buncombe Co. to North Carolina Electric Power dam on N.C. 191

Drop	Difficulty	Distance	Time	Scenery	Water Quality
83'	1-2	17 mi.	6.5 hrs.	A-B-C	Fair

Difficulties   There is a 10' dam at the end of the section. Take out below dam by carrying on the left and ferrying across to the right bank.

(6)   North Carolina Electric Power dam at N.C. 191 north of Asheville at Woodfin to Buncombe Co. Rt. 1634 bridge

Drop	Difficulty	Distance	Time	Scenery	Water Quality
130'	2-3	6.5 mi.	2 hrs.	A-B	Fair to Poor

Difficulties   Below the dam the current picks up speed as the river begins to drop over a series of ledges and heavier shoals. On the far right about 1 mi. below the dam, a Class 3 chute with heavy water presents the experienced paddler with an exciting run. This can be by-passed by working through the rock gardens in the center. With the increased gradient and

widening of the river, this section can become quite difficult in higher water. The Metro. Sewage Treatment Plant empties just below the put in, which might give one added incentive to stay upright.

(7) Buncombe Co. Rt. 1643 bridge at Alexander to dam at Marshall in Madison Co.

Drop	Difficulty	Distance	Time	Scenery	Water Quality
140'	1-2	11.5 mi.	4.5 hrs.	A-B	Fair to Poor

Difficulties   The 8' dam at the end of this section can present problems, so if taking out it would be best to pull out on the right bank in the vicinity of the intersection of N.C. 213 and U.S. Business 25-70, which will cut about .5 mi. off the trip. If continuing, a carry of some 400 yds. to below Rt. 1001 bridge will be necessary due to the bulkhead built along the banks below the dam.

(8) Madison Co. Rt. 1001 bridge in Marshall to Madison Co. Rt. 1151 bridge

Drop	Difficulty	Distance	Time	Scenery	Water Quality
100'	2	6.5 mi.	3 hrs.	A	Fair

Difficulties   About 1.5 mi. below Marshall, a 25 ft. dam should be approached quite cautiously. A carry of some 200 yds. on the right side is necessary. Beyond the dam the river continues with a constant gradient presenting the paddler with steady Class 2 water and practically no flat water. Those running this section only who don't wish to portage the dam can put in below the dam and above Rt. 1135 bridge on the right bank. This leaves a trip of some 5 mi.

(9) Madison Co. Rt. 1151 bridge at Barnard to U.S. 70-25 bridge in Hot Springs

Drop	Difficulty	Distance	Time	Scenery	Water Quality
210'	3-4/5	7.5 mi.	3 hrs.	A	Fair

Gage   Call (615) 525-5751 for a recorded report from TVA. A reading of 4,000 c.f.s. is maximum for open boats.

French Broad

Difficulties   The increased gradient combined with greater width and heavier water makes for an exciting trip through this section. Scouting becomes very difficuilt but quite necessary. For those who don't have a very dependable eddy turn in their repertoire, this simply "ain't the place to be." Generally the rule to follow is to stay to the left of all islands of any size.

There are seven major rapids in this section, all of which should be approached cautiously. The third of these rapids, "Big Pillow," will be found on the left side. The main flow of the river runs left, as the right side is clogged with boulders. The entrance rapid, a fast chute, flows diagonally left and requires the boater to fight to get back to the right in order to get by the large pillow and souse hole below it. There is, however, a narrow chute on the immediate left of the pillow, which can be negotiated in the event one ends up too far to the right. Both the entrance and the pillow should be scouted carefully. "Big Pillow" is located approximately 1.5 mi. below the put in. The next two rapids should be scouted on the left and right, respectively.

The community of Stackhouse, located approximately halfway through the section, can be recognized by the second island on the right. From this island a row of iron rods extends diagonally upstream about 2/3 of the way across the river. Move to the far left as soon as the island is observed. These rods can be seen at levels below 4,000 c.f.s.

Big Laurel Creek joins the French Broad about .25 mi. downstream from Stackhouse. Another .75 mi. downstream is Needle Rock, a sliver of shining rock located on the left bank high above the island separating the main channel. The main channel, which is on the left, has big standing waves which can easily swamp an open boat. It can be best scouted from the island. A small protected chute just left of the island drops rather quickly but can be run without too much danger.

The next large island in the middle of the river below Needle Rock will indicate the Class 5 and the last rapid of any consequence on the section. The rapid on the right has become known as "Frank Bell's Rapid" by canoeists in the area.* It consists of 3 concentric ledges which funnel the river into a giant whirlpool at the bottom. The passage to the left of the island is safest but certainly not unexciting. Both sides can be best scouted from the island.

* Frank Bell, owner of Camp Mondamin in Tusedo, N.C., was fortunate enough to be around at a time before dams were the answer to all problems. He ran the French Broad from its headwaters to the Gulf of Mexico. An attempt to run down the right side ended with his canoe remaining in the whirlpool for some 10 minutes, with him getting out after great difficulty.

French Broad

(10)   U.S. 70-25 bridge to U.S. 70-25 bridge in Tennessee

Drop	Difficulty	Distance	Time	Scenery	Water Quality
150'	2-3	13 mi.	4.5 hrs.	A-AA	Fair

Difficulties   At normal water levels there are several rapids where standing waves build up enough to give tandem paddlers problems. All can be "sneaked" by scouting carefully and generally staying to the inside on the bends. Below the second railroad bridge there is a 4' ledge that can be best run on the far left. Around the next bend there is a rapid, running some 75 yds., which one should approach cautiously on the right, and run on the right. At medium to high levels a giant eddy is formed between this rapid and the next ledge downstream, which is a natural dam. It should be scouted—left or right—and be given the same respect one should any dam. There are breaks that can be run, but hydraulics are formed at higher levels.

Directions   Practically all put ins and take outs are located on main arteries or in towns included on state maps, so no further explanations will be given here.

Take Out—On the east bank beneath U.S. 70-25 bridge, in Cocke Co., Tenn.

A fine detailed map of the French Broad from Rosman, N.C., to Newport, Tenn., is available for 75¢ from: River Guide, Land of Sky Regional Council, P.O. Box 2175, Asheville, N.C. 28802.

French Broad

French Broad, North Fork

The North Fork of the French Broad heads up on the eastern edge of the Nantahala National Forest. Its protected watershed gives it outstanding water quality. There are several beautiful waterfalls in the mile or so above the put in point, which the visitor to the area should attempt to see. This will prepare one for the beautifully rugged gorge to follow.

Topo Map   Rosman

County   Transylvania

(1)   Rt. 1326 bridge to U.S. 64 bridge

Drop	Difficulty	Distance	Timw	Scenery	Water Quality
390' 1 @ 145'/mi.	4-5/2@6	7.2 mi.	4.5 hrs.	AA	Excellent

Gage   U.S. 64 bridge on the south side of center piling. Minimum solo run at bottom of "0." Due to the gradient and constricted bed a level of 3" above the bottom of "0" would be a maximum level for a safe trip. Runnable during the spring and during or after rains.

Difficulties At the end of the first mile there is a 12 ft. fall, which is followed by a Class 3. Carry on the left of the falls.
About .5 mi. beyond is a Class 4, consisting of a very narrow chute with a hard left turn. Beyond here be on the lookout for the second falls, which are approximately 30 ft. high. Portage on old railroad bed on the right. The river begins dropping here at a rate approaching 145'/mi. through the third mile, and continues at a 95'/mi. rate through the fourth and a portion of the fifth mile.
A Class 6 follows the falls and 100 yds. downstream a second Class 6 razorback, which might necessitate a total portage of 150 yds.
Beyond the razorback a Class 5 runs 150 yds. while dropping about 20 ft. through a boulder field.
A third falls, 25 ft. high, will require a portage on the railroad bed, which is now on the left. Below the last falls Class 2 and 3 water runs for a mile before flattening out to a "calm" gradient of 25 ft./mi. for the final stretch.
This is a trip for the well conditioned paddler, and one that will be well worth the effort required.

Directions   **Put In**—North on Rt. 1321 off U.S. 64, 1 mi. west of Rosman.
Go west on 1326.
Take Out—U.S. 64 bridge, 1.1. mi. west of Rosman.

■

A man's life should be constantly fresh as this river. It should be the same channel, but a new water instant. Most men have no inclination, no rapids, no cascades, but marshes, and alligators, and miasma instead.

Thoreau, *A Week on the Concord and Merrimac Rivers*

French Broad, North Fork

Green River

Green River

The Green drops through a great boulder-strewn gorge after leaving Lake Summit, until it crosses into Polk County. After leaving the deep gorge and entering Polk, it levels out into a delightful fast flowing stream cutting between Cove and Chimney Top mountains on the south and McCraw Mountain to the north. Through this area is it a fairly small stream dropping over small ledges and through small rock gardens. The area is sparsely settled, but evidence of encroaching civilization is growing fast.

Next to the Nantahala, the Green is probably canoed more than any other river in North Carolina. During the summer months hardly a day passes without seeing two or three groups of canoeists from various summer camps holding classes there. It is an excellent stream for teaching the basics of river canoeing.

This popularity has created problems for people who live in the Cove. On summer weekends dust hangs in the air as shuttles race up and down the river road; beer bottles and cans are strewn about; and nudity is flaunted. This is a nice place to visit, but not as nice to live in as it might be. It is hoped that the establishment of the Green as a State Natural/Scenic River will alleviate these problems.

At this time there is limited parking on the side of the road through the Cove. It is patrolled regularly—especially on weekends. An early arrival is recommended in order to get into the parking area. Duke Power Company is assisting in this project in an attempt to lessen the impact of the heavy traffic.

Topo Maps   Cliffield Mtn., Lake Lure, Rutherfordton South

Counties   Polk and Rutherford (Broad)

(1)   Rt. 1151 (Green Cove Rd.) to where the river leaves the road

Drop	Difficulty	Distance	Time	Scenery	Water Quality
126'	2-3	6 mi.	2.5 hrs.	A-B	Good

Gage   None. This is a dam-controlled stream and is runnable only when the plant in Tuxedo, N.C. is operating. Generally under normal conditions the plant operates during the week, in which case water arrives at the put in each day about 1 p.m. Call (803) 583-8406 to check out the schedule of operation on weekends, holidays, or during extreme dry spells.

Green River

Difficulties   Green Cove Rd. follows along the river the entire distance, making scouting rather easy. The first rapid of any consequence is "Big Corky" (1.3 rd. mi. below the first bridge) which can be recognized by the quiet pool above it and the sandy beach on the left below it. When both turbines are running it presents a nice standing wave to douse the bowman in.

A second rapid about .25 mi. below "Big Corky" can present problems to the unwary paddler. It bears to the left and drops over a rock bed for about 75 yds. Farther downstream a series of ledges running for some 200 yds. should be approached cautiously. The road is high above the river at this point.

The approach to "Little Corky," a low Class 3, occurs just beyond a point where the road has dropped down to the river and a sizeable island separates the main stream. The more difficult run is on the left of the island. It drops fast with an apparent straight chute off the right bank. One rock barely under water is the grabber awaiting the straight shooter. A slight movement to the left will shoot the canoe between it and a similar rock on the left. They are little more than a canoe width apart. Scout on the left.

Below "Little Corky" the river continues to drop fast for .5 mi., then it slows down somewhat. Primarily fun water following the last "Corky."

Directions   **Put In**—Off I-40 at Saluda Exit, go east approximately 300 yds. to Green Cove Rd. (Rt. 1151), and left down a series of hairpin curves to where the road straightens. The river is on the left. Turn into the first pull-off on the left. This puts one above a fast water rapid, requiring some quick maneuvering.

Put In—From Mill Spring (N.C.) take N.C. 9 north about 100 yds., then go west on Rt. 1138 to Silver Creek Baptist Church. Turn left on Rt. 1151 to the river. Proceed to the point where the road starts up the mountain and turn right into the parking lot.

Take Out—6.3 rd. mi. from the put in parking area to the second parking area, located just beyond a point where one loses sight of the river.

The following sections have been included for those who might like to take a more leisurely float trip, or who might be looking for quieter waters for overnighters. If one wishes an extended trip beyond the reaches of the Green, see sections (4) through (10) on the Broad.

94

(2) N.C. 9 below Lake Adger Dam to Polk Co. Rt. 1311

Drop	Difficulty	Distance	Time	Scenery	Water Quality
52'	1-2	7 mi.	2.5 hrs.	A-B	Good

Gage None. When the upper Green is running, generally the dam at Adger will be generating, thus giving a very nice water level.

Difficulties None, but beware of downed trees.

(3) Polk Co. Rt. 1311 to N.C. 1005

Drop	Difficulty	Distance	Time	Scenery	Water Quality
38'	1-2	10.2 mi.	4.5 hrs.	A-B	Good

Gage See Section (2).

Difficulties None.

(4) N.C. 1005 to N.C. 1004 on the Broad River

Drop	Difficulty	Distance	Time	Scenery	Water Quality
26'	1	6.7 mi.	3 hrs.	A-B	Good

Gage See Section (2).

Difficulties None.

Take Out—Southeast approximately 11.5 mi. from Mill Spring to N.C. 1004, then north to the river.

We used to joke occasionally about setting the shuttle on the wrong river—always considering such below our level of intelligence. In this area the impossible can happen. On the first trip by the author on section (1) of the Broad we arrived at the take out only to find no vehicle. Same story at the next bridge. Here we were, mid March and cold, and getting more so with the sun setting and no transportation. Well, logic finally prevailed and we found our shuttle after a 5 mi. walk in the dark—not on the Broad, but on the Green.

Swannanoa River

The Swannonoa drops off the western slopes of the Blue Ridge at Swannanoa Gap, just east of the town of Black Mountain. It remains fairly small and narrow until joined by the North Fork, east of Swannanoa.

It flows through wooded areas and farmland, much of which is owned by Warren Wilson College, before passing under U.S. 70 and through an industrial area in Asheville. It joins the French Broad in the city limits.

Bob Watts, of Black Mountain, has been a one man "Save the Swannanoa" gang in trying to clean up the river and keep it clear for canoeing. Every stream needs a friend like Bob.

Topo Map   Oteen

County   Buncombe

(1)   Main bridge in Swannanoa (above Mr. Zip) to the U.S. 70 bridge at Azalea

Drop	Difficulty	Distance	Time	Scenery	Water Quality
135'	1-2	8.6 mi.	4 hrs.	A-B-C	Good

Gage   On the southwest side of the bridge by Mr. Zip. Minimum for solo is 4" below "0." Can be run at 6" below "0" from Charles D. Owen Park. Generally there is adequate water to run during the spring through mid June and during wet seasons.

Difficulties   Always be on the lookout for downed trees.

There is a sewer pipe across the river at the upper end of Charles D. Owen Park. At water levels at the bottom of "0" and above, the paddler won't be able to run under it. Move right quickly and portage.

Just below the park there are several small islands with narrow channels. The one main channel can easily be blocked by downed trees. Proceed carefully.

Directions   **Put In**—On the north side of the river about 50 yds. below the bridge. There is adequate parking along the shoulder here. Please don't use the lot at Mr. Zip for parking.

To Charles D. Owen Park (Buncombe Co. Parks and Recreation Dept.) bear right on Farm School Rd. off old 70 from the main bridge in Swannanoa. Put

Swannanoa River

in at the lower end of the park. A small road runs to within a few yards of the river. It would probably be best to park cars at the main lot after unloading. Putting in here will shorten the trip by about 2 mi.

      Take Out—On the southeast side of U.S. 70 bridge at Azalea. Opposite Azalea Methodist Church.

Section 3

Section 3

Buck Creek

Buck Creek has its headwaters in the Mt. Mitchell Wildlife Management Area below the Blue Ridge Parkway. It flows along N.C. 80 into Lake Tahoma. Above the lake it is a small, fast dropping stream while below it flattens out somewhat, flowing over small ledges and rocks.

Topo Map   Marion

County   McDowell

(1)   Lake Tahoma Dam to U.S. 70

Drop	Difficulty	Distance	Time	Scenery	Water Quality
72'	1-2	3.2 mi.	1.5 hrs.	A-B	Good

Gage   U.S. 70 on northeast side of bridge. Minimum for solo run is reading of 6'' below "0." Buck Creek drains a small area and can be run in later winter, spring, and following rain.

Difficulties   None, but fast maneuvering will be required in several tight passages.

Directions   **Put In**—Turn off Rt. 80 on the first road below the dam. There is little space for turning around at the end of this road.
Take Out—East side of U.S. 70 bridge just east of the community of Pleasant Gardens.

Buck Creek

Buffalo Creek

The Buffalo flows from the junction of several small streams in Buffalo Cove. It courses through a small valley until it cuts through a deep remote gorge. After leaving the gorge it comes back along the highway before leveling out slightly as it confluences with the Yadkin. The Buffalo throughout its course is a small low water stream flowing over gravel bars with a few small ledges.

Topo Map   Bufaflo Cove

County   Caldwell

(1)   Rt. 1503 bridge to N.C. 268 bridge

Drop	Difficulty	Distance	Time	Scenery	Water Quality
180'	2/3	6 mi.	3 hrs.	A-B	Good-Fair

Gage   On Rt. 1505 low water bridge on the northwest side. Go to water level on the northeast side to read. A minimum level of 6" below "0" is required for solo. Rt. 1505 is the first road on the right off Rt. 1504 after leaving N.C. 268. The best water level will be obtained during the spring and following runoffs from rain.

Difficulties   There are two broken dams on this section, the first of which is located in the first gorge the stream enters below the put in. The chute appears open but a large rock and an iron bar which are barely under the surface can easily damage a boat attempting to pass through.

The second dam, about 10 ft. high, can be seen from Rt. 1505 bridge where the gage is located. It should be approached very carefully when the water is high enough to be flowing over the top. It can be portaged on the left bank.

Directions   **Put In**—Northeast of Patterson on N.C. 268, north of Rt. 1504 to Rt. 1503.
Take Out—The junction of Buffalo Creek with the Yadkin River about 50 yds. from N.C. 168 bridge over the Yadkin.

Catawba River

Catawba River

The Catawba heads up above Catawba Falls in the extreme western portion of McDowell County and flows into Lake James north of Marion. Below Linville Dam on Lake James, it continues until it reaches the backwaters of Lake Rhodhiss. After Lake Rhodhiss the river is impounded several times with little fast free flowing water, therefore the reason for no further description.

The river is small and fast in section (1), but carries industrial pollution east of Old Fort. Except for this it could be a very pretty run. However, there are several areas where gravel operations are evident.

Below Lake James the river flows primarily through woodlands until it reaches Morganton.

Topo Maps   Marion, Glen Alpine, Morganton South, Morganton North

Counties   McDowell, Burke

(1)   McDowell Co. Rt. 1234 bridge to U.S. 221 bridge

Drop	Difficulty	Distance	Time	Scenery	Water Quality
85'	1-2	12 mi.	6 hrs.	B-C	Poor

Gage   Southside of Rt. 1234 bridge. Minimum level for solo paddling is 6" below "0." Can be run year round except during extreme dry seasons.

Difficulties   There are several series of ledges, the first of which is below the confluence of Crooked Creek on the right. This one in particular should be scouted. An earlier take out can be made along McDowell Rt. 1214 for those who desire a shorter run.

Directions   **Put In**—Catawba Rt. 1234 off I-40 east of Old Fort (at the Parker Padgett Rd. exit).
Take Out—U.S. 221 bridge north of Marion.

(2)   Burke Co. Rt. 1223 bridge to Rt. 1147 bridge

Drop	Difficulty	District	Time	Scenery	Water Quality
41'	1-2	8.5 mi.	3 hrs.	B	Good

Catawba River

Gage   None. The power plant is operating if there are no significant
           mud flats along the banks. This will provide plenty of water.
When it is not in operation the first two gravel bars in section (2) probably will
need to be walked. Afte these two the remainder can be negotiated.

Difficulties The volume of water coming from the Bridgewater Plant of
             Duke Power Company is completely unpredictable. This pre-
sents a situation where the water level increases approximately two feet within
a matter of seconds and can be rather dangerous in the first 200 yds. below
the put in, particularly so 50 yds. downstream, where a large tree blocks most
of the channel on the right. Put in on the left of the bridge to be safe. The
stretch above the second bridge has several islands that should be approached
carefully when the water is up.

(3) Burke Co. Rt. 1147 bridge (Watermill Rd.) to N.C. 18 bridge

Drop	Difficulty	Distance	Time	Scenery	Water Quality
17′	1	7.5 mi.	3 hrs.	A-B	Good

Gage   See section (2).

Difficulties None. However, when the plant is in operation the increased
             volume adds to the difficulty for the novice.

Directions **Put In—(Section 2)** Burke Co. Rt. 1223 bridge west of Glen Al-
            pine and 400 yds. east of Bridgewater Power Plant at Lake
            James.
            Take Out—(Section 3) N.C. 18 bridge north of Morganton on
            south bank at gravel pit.

■

*The movement of a canoe is like a reed in the wind. Silence is part of it, and
the sounds of lapping water, bird songs, and wind in the trees. It is part of the
medium through which it floats, the sky, the water, and the shores. A man is
part of his canoe and therefore part of all it knows. The instant he dips his
paddle, he flows as it flows, the canoe yielding to his slightest touch and
responsive to his every whim and thought. . . .*

                                                        Sigurd F. Olson

Catawba River, North Fork

The North Fork has its headwaters on Humpback Mountain below the Blue Ridge Parkway. It is a small shallow stream which U.S. 221 follows down the mountain, until Armstrong Creek comes in and it picks up considerably. Also, in the Sevier area it receives some degree of industrial pollution. Below Sevier it enters a small gorge and continues on its way to Lake James. The river runs parallel to and below the western ridge of the Linville Gorge Wilderness Area. With the exception of the Clinchfield Railroad running along the east bank for about half way down, this is an uninhabited area. It remains fairly narrow as it courses over ledges and through small boulder gardens.

Topo Maps   Little Switzerland, Marion East

County   McDowell

(1)   On McDowell Co. Rt. 1559 to Rt. 1552 bridge

Drop	Difficulty	Distance	Time	Scenery	Water Quality
160'	2-3	5.6 mi.	3.5 hrs.	A	Good

Gage   On northwest side of railroad bridge at put in; minimum level for solo is 2" below "0."
Can generally be run during wet seasons or immediately after a rain. Run off will be fast.

Difficulties   600 yds. below the put in a boulder garden runs about 100 yds. This will require a great deal of maneuvering. It would be best to scout on the right bank.
There are several interesting rapids before arriving at the railroad bridge, but below it an 8 ft. slanting falls should be approached with caution. Three 2 to 3 ft. ledges follow it closely. Run on the right. The river drops about 16' within 150 yds. through this area. Scout on the right bank again.
With a reading of approximately 4" above the bottom of "0" on the gage, several of the rapids will require scouting.

Directions   Put In—North of Marion on U.S. 221 to Woodlawn, then east on Rt. 1556 to Rt. 1559 and 100 yds. to put in on river's edge, between the creek bridge and railroad bridge.

Take Out—North of Marion on U.S. 221. East on Rt. 1501 (Hankins Rd.) to Burnett's Landing. Turn left on Rt. 1552 to the bridge. A slightly easier take out can be made at the Wildlife Access Area .5 mi. downstream from Rt. 1552 bridge. Look for the sign on the right, after passing Burnett's Landing.

Catawba River, North Fork

Henry Fork River

Henry Fork River

The Henry Fork heads up in the South Mountains and flows east out of Burke County into Catawba County, where it meets the Jacob Fork and forms the South Fork Catawba River. The first 15 mi. flow through an area abounding in laurel and rhododendron, making a very scenic run. The stretches below are generally flat and include two dams. Also, sewage is pumped into the river below the dam at Brookford.

Topo Maps Morganton South, Valdese, Longview, Hickory

Counties Burke, Catawba

(1) Burke Rt. 1919 bridge south of Enola to Rt. 1916 bridge

Drop	Difficulty	Distance	Time	Scenery	Water Quality
160'	2-3	4.4 mi.	2 hrs.	A-B	Good

Gage On the south side of N.C. 18 bridge. Reading at the bottom of 1 for solo run through first 2.3 mi. to Rt. 1922 bridge; 4" below "0" from 1922 to 1916 is a minimum. Run only after rain.

Difficulties None that are dangerous, but a constant gradient of 48'/mi. through the first 2.5 mi. will demand great caution through here. This section consists of many small ledges which are generally followed by pools.

(2) Burke Rt. 1916 bridge, just off Rt. 1924 (old N.C. 18), to Rt. 1916 bridge

Drop	Difficulty	Distance	Time	Scenery	Water Quality
74'	1-2	5 mi.	2.5 hrs.	A	Good

Gage 4" below "0" minimum for solo. Run most of the year except dry seasons.

Difficulties None. Primarily shallows and small shoals.

(3) Burke Rt. 1916 bridge (second bridge below the put in on section (2)) to N.C. 18 bridge

Drop	Difficulty	Distance	Time	Scenery	Water Quality
92′	1-2/3	5.2 mi.	2.5 hrs.	A-B	Good

Gage 2″ below top of "0" minimum for solo. Run late winter, spring or after rain.

Difficulties There are several shoals which drop quickly. The Class 3 consists of a series of staircase ledges which continue for 125 yds. and necessitate a lot of maneuvering.

(4) N.C. 18 bridge to Rt. 1803 bridge

Drop	Difficulty	Distance	Time	Scenery	Water Quality
43′	1-2	4.9 mi.	2 hrs.	B-C	Good to Fair

Gage 6″ below "0" minimum for solo run. Run year round except during extremely dry spells.

Difficulties One small rock garden.

(5) Burke Rt. 1803 bridge to N.C. 127 bridge

Drop	Difficulty	Distance	Time	Scenery	Water Quality
70′	1-2	7.6 mi.	3 hrs.	B	Fair

Gage 6″ below "0." Run year round.

Difficulties A 20 ft. dam at the Henry River Mills, just below Catawba Rt. 1002 bridge, requires a portage of 150 yds. on the left side around the mill.

(6) N.C. 127 bridge at Brookford to Catawba Rt. 1143 bridge

Drop	Difficulty	Distance	Time	Scenery	Water Quality
38′	1	6 mi.	2.5 hrs.	B	Fair to Poor

Gage

Difficulties A 30 ft. dam in the town of Brookford can be portaged on the right bank. Approach with caution.

Directions   **Put In**—Take the Enola Rd. south off I-40 at the Western Carolina exit in Morganton. Proceed to Rt. 1918, the first paved road
to the right beyond the community of Enola, and continue to end of pavement.

Take Out—N.C. 127 south, off U.S. 64-70, to Brookford; south
on Catawba Rt. 1008 to Rt. 1144, then east to the bridge.

Henry Fork River

Jacob Fork River

Jacob Fork River

The Jacob Fork flows out of the South Mountains through an area of rolling hills, until it confluences with the Henry Fork. Most of the sections listed are closed in, with little signs of habitation except in the immediate areas around the bridges. The banks generally abound in laurel and rhododendron.

Topo Maps   Casar, Banoak, Longview, Hickory

Counties   Burke, Catawba

(1)   Burke Co. Rt. 1901 bridge to N.C. 18 bridge

Drop	Difficulty	Distance	Time	Scenery	Water Quality
136'	1-2	9.2 mi.	3 hrs.	B	Good

Gage   U.S.G.S. gage at Burke Co. Rt. 1924 bridge (old N.C. 18). Minimum for solo is 2.75. Can be run most of the year except during dry spells.

Difficulties   In the horseshoe bend between Burke Co. Rt. 1907 bridge and 1910 bridge there are remains of a 10 ft. dam. Approach very cautiously in higher water levels. Portage on the left.

(2)   N.C. 18 bridge to Catawba Co. Rt. 1116 bridge

Drop	Difficulty	Distance	Time	Scenery	Water Quality
145'	1-2	12.2 mi.	4.5 hrs.	A-B	Fair

Gage   U.S.G.S. gage. Minimum for solo is 2.0. Gage also on N.C. 127 bridge on northwest side. Minimum for solo is 4" below "0."

Difficulties   None

(3)   Catawba Co. Rt. 1116 bridge to Rt. 1139 bridge

Drop	Difficulty	Distance	Time	Scenery	Water Quality
82'	1-2	7.4 mi.	2.5 hrs.	A-B	Good to Fair

Gage   N.C. 127 bridge. Minimum for solo is 4" below "0."

Difficulties   None

Directions   **Put In**—Burke Co. Rt. 1924 (old N.C. 18) south of Morganton approximately 12 mi., then west on Rt. 1901 to bridge.
Take Out—Catawba Rt. 1139 bridge, then 3.1 mi. north of N.C. 10 (south of Hickory).

■

There is magic in the feel of a paddle and the movement of a canoe, a magic compounded of distance, adventure, solitude and peace. The way of a canoe is the way of the wilderness and of a freedom almost forgotten, the open door to waterways of ages past and a way of life with profound and abiding satisfactions.
                                                                    Sigurd F. Olson

Johns River

The Johns heads up in the Globe area of the Pisgah National Forest. It wanders through farm land and wooded areas until it reaches the backwaters of Duke Power Company's Lake Rhodhiss, north of Morganton. A gap, between sections (1) and (2), has been left due to the many low water bridges located through that stretch.

Topo Maps   Globe, Collettsville, Morganton North

Counties   Burke, Caldwell

(1)   Johns River Camp Bridge to second low water bridge after leaving N.C. 90.

Drop	Difficulty	Distance	Time	Scenery	Water Quality
115'	1-2	4.5 mi.	2.5 hrs.	B	Excellent

Gage   East side of Caldwell Co. Rt. 1337 bridge in Collettsville. Minimum for solo is 4" below "0." There is also a corresponding gage on the east side of Burke Co. Rt. 1438 bridge. With a level of 2" above the bottom of "0" the trip can be extended 3.5 mi. by putting in at Caldwell Co. Rt. 1367 low water bridge.

Difficulties   None, other than a couple of very tight passages which might be blocked by downed trees. Do not trespass on private property through here, which can prove rather difficult with some 7 low water bridges.

(2)   Caldwell Co. Rt. 1337 bridge in Collettsville to Rt. 1328 bridge

Drop	Difficulty	Distance	Time	Scenery	Water Quality
43'	1-2	6 mi.	2.5 hrs.	B	Good

Gage   Minimum for solo is 6" below "0."

Difficulties   One area below the old sand and gravel pit, which may be clogged with debris after high water.

Johns River

(3) Rt. 1328 low water bridge to Burke Co. Rt. 1438

Drop	Difficulty	Distance	Time	Scenery	Water Quality
38′	1-2	6.5 mi.	2.5 hrs.	B	Good

Gage   Minimum level for solo is 6″ below "0."

Difficulties   None.

(4) Burke Co. Rt. 1438 bridge (30 yds. upstream on east bank) to N.C. Wildlife Access Area at N.C. 18 bridge

Drop	Difficulty	Distance	Time	Scenery	Water Quality
12′	1	5.5 mi.	2.5 hrs.	B	Good

Gage   Minimum level for solo is 6″ below "0."

Difficulties   None.

Directions   **Put In—Section (1)** N.C. 90 north of Collettsville at Johns River United Church of Christ Camp bridge. Ask permission if the campground is open.
Take Out—Second low water bridge on Rt. 1356 southwest off N.C. 90.
Put In—Section (1) Rt. 1337 bridge at N.C. 90 in Collettsville.
Take Out—N.C. 18 bridge northwest of Morganton.

Tom Bolen and Les Bechdel train on the Nantahala.
Photo courtesy of the Nantahala Outdoor Center.

New River

The New begins with the confluence of the North and South Forks. At this point it has already become a fairly wide river although still primarily shallow (see section (6), South Fork, New River). From Mouth of Wilson to Stuart Dam the New is mostly flat, therefore the reason for omitting these 2.5 mi.

The river flows through forested rolling hills and pastoral lands and in general is a very scenic stream. We recommend Randy Carter's *Canoeing White Water* to those who wish to paddle further sections of the New to the north and into West Virginia.

Topo Maps Mouth of Wilson (Va.); Sparta West and Sparta East (N.C.-Va); Briarpatch Mtn. and Galax (Va.)

Counties Grayson (Va.); Alleghany (N.C.)

(1) Stuart Dam to U.S. 221 and 21 bridge

Drop	Difficulty	Distance	Time	Scenery	Water Quality
72′	1-2/3	11 mi.	4 hrs.	B	Good

Gage None, however the river can be run all year. The river has widened considerably and care should be taken if conditions are such that there might be high water.

Difficulties Downstream one mile from Grayson Co. 601 bridge in the community of Cox Chapel as the river bends to the right there are two rapids. The first, a long class 2, should be scouted from the left in higher water. The second, a couple of hundred yards beyond the first, is a class 3 where most of the water flows hard left by a large boulder on the bank. Watch for the drop just beyond the boulder. Attempt to scout on the right. At higher water levels this can be run in the center.

This area of the rapids is where Appalachian Power Company proposed to construct their dam (see South Fork, New River).

(2) U.S. 221 and 21 bridge to U.S. 58 and 221 bridge

Drop	Difficulty	Distance	Time	Scenery	Water Quality
125′	1-2	23.5 mi.	9 hrs.	A-B	Good

Gage None. Can be run year round.

Difficulties None. This is primarily flat with occasional riffles and a few shoals. This is a favorite float trip for canoe camping, especially for a two nighter.

Directions **Put In**—At Stuart Dam alongside U.S. 58 east of Mouth of Wilson.
Take Out—U.S. 58-221 bridge west of Galax, Va.

New River

New River

John Kennedy and Linda Aponte at the Nantahala River Nationals.
Photo courtesy of the Nantahala Outdoor Center.

North Fork, New River

The North Fork heads up in the extreme western end of Ashe County just over the Tennessee line. It flows northeast in the shadows of The Peak, Three Top Mountain, and Phoenix Mountain on the south before confluencing with the South Fork and forming the New River.

It is primarily a stream of shallow ledges with an occasional gravel bar through its upper reaches. Then it flattens out to where it presents a few riffles and a ledge now and then. River access is quite easy with roads following alongside most of the entire distance. This also gives it a pastoral setting through most of the sections.

It may be of interest to note that Ashe County has almost 110 miles of waters that are canoeable throughout most of the year.

Topo Maps   Baldwin Gap, Warrensville, Jefferson, Grassy Creek, Mouth of Wilson (Va.)

County   Ashe

(1)   Ashe Co. Rt. 1119 bridge at community of Maxwell to Rt. 1100 bridge

Drop	Difficulty	Distance	Time	Scenery	Water Quality
76'	1-2	6.8 mi.	3 hrs.	B	Excellent

Gage   On northeast piling of Rt. 1642 bridge (Rowie McNeil Rd). Minimum for solo is 4'' below "0." Can be run from Clifton down most of the year except during extremely dry seasons.

Difficulties   A series of gravel bars in the first 1.5 mi. which drop at a rate of about 25 ft./mi.

(2)   Rt. 1100 bridge at Creston to N.C. 88 bridge

Drop	Difficulty	Distance	Time	Scenery	Water Quality
85'	1	7.2 mi.	3 hrs.	B	Good

Gage   Minimum for solo is 6'' below "0."

Difficulties   None, but watch for low water bridges.

North Fork, New River

36°20'

(3) N.C. 88 bridge west of Clifton to Rt. 1644 bridge

Drop	Difficulty	Distance	Time	Scenery	Water Quality
89'	1-2	11 mi.	4.5 hrs.	A-B	Good

Gage　　Minimum for solo is 6" below "0."

Difficulties　Below Clifton where the river bends sharply away from N.C. 88 and then back, there is a 12 ft. dam which can be seen from the highway. Carry on the left. There is a 4 ft. slanting ledge immediately below the dam which can be run with a couple of inches above the minimum. Watch for low water bridges.

(4) Rt. 1644 low water bridge (Bernard Miller Rd.) to N.C. 16 bridge

Drop	Difficulty	Distance	Time	Scenery	Water Quality
101'	1-2	10 mi.	4 hrs.	A-B	Good

Gage　　Minimum for solo is 6" below "0."

Difficulties　None other than a few gravel bars.

(5) N.C. 16 bridge to Ashe Co. Rt. 1549 and Alleghany Rt. 1311 below the confluence with the South Fork.

Drop	Difficulty	Distance	Time	Scenery	Water Quality
126'	1-2	8 mi.	3.5 hrs.	A-B	Fair

Gage　　Minimum for solo is 7" below "0."

Difficulties　Below the first bridge after the put in there are the remains of a washed out low water bridge that will require portaging at normal water levels. Carry or scout on the left.

One low water bridge farther downstream should be approached with caution at higher levels.

Directions　**Put In**—West on N.C. 88 to Ashe Co. Rt. 1119, and south to the bridge.

Take Out—East on Ashe Co. Rt. 1535 off N.C. 16 (just south of Va. state line) to Rt. 1549 along the New River.

North Fork, New River

South Fork, New River

The South Fork begins at the confluence of several small streams southeast of Boone, meanders across the three most northwesterly counties in North Carolina before joining the North Fork and forming the New just south of the Virginia line. It is primarily an easy flowing stream over rocky beds, with occasional riffles·as it threads its way between mountains on one side and fields on the other. The South Fork is an excellent stream for canoe camping, even though there are low water bridges on practically every section that will generally require carrying.

The forks, as well as the New itself, were known as the Teays River on maps showing ancient rivers, and at one time was the master water system of North America. The New cuts north and west across Virginia into West Virginia, where it is joined by the Gauley and becomes the Kanawha.

The river, perhaps the oldest in the country, appeared to be short lived when plans for a giant hydroelectric plant were firming up in the early seventies. Two dams were planned which would have flooded some 42,000 acres, mostly in North Carolina. After a long hard battle which gathered national support, the river was saved when President Ford signed a bill on September 11, 1976 establishing a 26.5 mi. section as a National Wild and Scenic River. This section consists of 22 mi. of the South Fork plus the first 4.5 mi. of the main stem (most of sections (5) and (6)).

Naturally this has brought an influx of paddlers to the river—especially on the Wild and Scenic section, which quite often has resulted in property damage and hard feelings by residents. Perhaps we can keep this in mind when floating here.

Topo Maps   Mouth of Wilson, Briarpath Mts., and Galax (Va.); Sparta West and Sparta East (N.C.-Va.)

Counties   Watauga, Ashe, Alleghany (N.C.); Grayson (Va.)

(1)   U.S. 421 bridge to Watauga Rt. 1347

Drop	Difficulty	Distance	Time	Scenery	Water Quality
110'	1	18 mi.	6 hrs.	A-B	Fair

Gage   U.S.G.S. gage is on the right bank 200 yds. upstream of N.C. 16 and 88. Minimum for solo is 2.50. Gage on U.S. 221-441 on southwest side. Minimum for solo is 5" below "0." The river below Todd can be run year round. It would be wise to check the gage during spells of extreme

South Fork, New River

South Fork, New River

dryness to determine the advisability of running the upper section in particular.

Difficulties   None, other than low water bridges and shallow gravel bars at lower water levels. There are, however, many low overhanging branches.

(2)   Watauga Rt. 1347 just south of intersection with Ashe Rt. 1100 in Todd to low water bridge in Fleetwood

Drop	Difficulty	Distance	Time	Scenery	Water Quality
85'	1-2	10 mi.	4.5 hrs.	A-B	Good

Gage   U.S.G.S. minimum for solo is 2.40. Gage on U.S. 221-441. Minimum is 6" below "0."

Difficulties   None, other than low water bridges. One set of shoals about 2 mi. above the take out.

(3)   Low water bridge in Fleetwood (below cemetery on hill) off Ashe Rt. 1106 to N.C. 163 bridge

Drop	Difficulty	Distance	Time	Scenery	Water Quality
101'	1-2	17 mi.	6 hrs.	A-B	Good

Gage   U.S.G.S. minimum is 2.40. Gage on U.S. 221-441. Minimum is 6" below "0."

Difficulties   None, other than low water bridges.

(4)   N.C. 163 bridge to N.C. 88 and 16 bridge

Drop	Difficulty	Distance	Time	Scenery	Water Quality
98'	1-2	14 mi.	5 hrs.	A-B	Good

Gage   U.S.G.S. minimum is 2.40. Gage on U.S. 221-441. Minimum is 6" below "0."

Difficulties   The usual low water bridges. A series of shoals begin about 2 mi. below the put in and continue to the entrance to the Methodist Campground along the right bank. The camp does have

South Fork, New River

an area for family camping which the paddler passes along the river. It is available for a reasonable fee during the spring and summer.

(5) N.C. 88 and 16 bridge at Index (at Walter Sheet's Grocery) to U.S. 221 bridge

Drop	Difficulty	Distance	Time	Scenery	Water Quality
118'	1-2	15 mi.	5 hrs.	A-B	Good

Gage   U.S.G.S. gage. Minimum is 2.30.

Difficulties   None, other than low water bridges.

(6) U.S. 221 bridge to Mouth of Wilson, Va.

Drop	Difficulty	Distance	Time	Scenery	Water Quality
144'	1-2	15 mi.	5.5 hrs.	A-B	Good

Gage   U.S.G.S. gage minimum is 2.30.

Difficulties   A series of shoals above the confluence with the North Fork runs for over 200 yds. After entering the New there is a series just above Mouth of Wilson. The trip can be shortened about 5 mi. by taking out below the confluence on Alleghany Rt. 1311 and Ashe Rt. 1549.

Directions   **Put In**—U.S. Rt. 421 bridge south of Boone.
Take Out—Grayson Co. Rt. 716 and Alleghany Co. Rt. 1313 south of Mouth of Wilson, Va. South on Grayson 767 off U.S. 58 and left on Rt. 716.

South Fork, New River

Nolichucky River

Below the confluence of the Toe and Cane Rivers the Nolichucky is born—not as a small, gurgling trickle but as a full grown, boisterous, fast flowing river. Down from Poplar the river enters Cherokee National Forest while cutting a gorge 800-1,000 ft. deep between the Bald Mountains on the south and the Unaka Mountains on the north. The Clinchfield Railroad follows the river through the entire gorge. For those who would like to enjoy the rugged grandeur of the gorge and the river to the fullest, hiking is the way. The paddler can only enjoy the river, for it gives one little opportunity to view the magnificent scenery above. The river has many long rapids with heavy water, which offer little opportunity for rescue. This is a river for the advanced canoeist.

Section (2), although not as spectacular, offers the paddler outstanding scenery with such rock formations as Devil's Looking Glass.

Topo Maps   Huntdale (N.C.); Unicoi, Erwin (Tenn.)

Counties   Mitchell (N.C.); Unicoi, Washington (Tenn.)

(1)   Poplar, N.C. to Erwin, Tenn.

Drop	Difficulty	Distance	Time	Scenery	Water Quality
338' .5 mi. @ 66'/mi.	3-4-5	11.5 mi.	7 hrs.	A-A	Fair

Gage   Call T.V.A. (615) 525-5751 for a 24 hr. recorded message on stream flow. A flow of 500 c.f.s. is a minimum, while 2,000 c.f.s. can be considered a maximum.

Difficulties   The first rapid below the railroad bridge is about 75 yds. long, over a series of ledges. There is an open passage to right of center, but two large standing waves tend to swamp open boats in higher water. The next rapid, "On the Rocks," can be easily recognized. An attempt at running it may well prove why it's so named. A line of boulders on the right forces the main current through a narrow chute in the center. A hidden rock left of center blocks what normally appears as an open run through here. At about 1,200 c.f.s. the 4" vertical drop to the immediate left of the chute is runnable. Both of these rapids can be best scouted by pulling in at the railroad bridge and walking down the tracks. The time spent walking here can save a considerable amount that would be required to free a boat.

Nolichucky River

If the passage on each of the rapids which follow isn't immediately apparent, scout! Generally most of them can be run on the right side.

The third and fourth are series of ledges interspersed with boulders. The fourth, some 250 yds. long, ends up with a 4 ft. ledge. Run the chute on the far right at medium levels. Scout on the left.

The next major rapid, "Roostertail," lost some of its tail in the November 1977 flood, but remains a force to contend with. The water rushes through on the right and piles up against a large boulder at bottom right. At medium high levels it is best to work to the far left through the rock garden.

There is still plenty of action beyond here, but if the paddler has made it this far without major mishaps he can breathe a little easier. Most of the remaining rapids have passages that are easily recognized.

There is one, however, "The Sousehole," that should be approached very carefully. A creek enters the river through a culvert 10 ft. above the river on the left. Below it the river bears hard right by an island and then back to the left. Stay close to the left bank all the way around these two bends. At the bottom of the left bend one will find "The Sousehole." It's a nice place to pass and look in on but certainly not to visit.

Downstream the river continues to drop over a few ledges and through some stubble fields until it reaches the take out.

Directions   **Put In**—From Spruce Pine, N.C., take N.C. 226 to .1 mi. north of Red Hill; go west on Mitchell Co. 1304 to the river, then continue along it to Mitchell Co. 1321, then north and west approximately 5 mi. to Poplar. Cross the railroad tracks and bear left directly in front of Molly's Country Store. The U.S.G.S. gage is approximately 50 yds. downstream from the put in, on the right bank. This is a private landing, so do not abuse the privilege of using it. The Chief of Police of St. Augustine, Florida, constructed the steps to get to his summer home, which might be an added incentive to take care.

Take Out—West from Poplar on 1321, to 1323 (Forest Rd. 230) over Indian Grave Gap to state line and Tenn. Rt. 30, into Erwin. Go south on U.S. 19-W and 23 to Nolichucky bridge.

(2) U.S. 19W and 23 bridge south of Erwin to Tenn. Rt. 67 bridge

Drop	Difficulty	Distance	Time	Scenery	Water Quality
185'	2-3	11.8 mi.	5.5 hrs.	A	Fair

Gage   U.S.G.S. gage is located on west side, 100 yds. upstream of Tenn. 81 bridge at Embreeville. A medium level would be a reading of about 2.40. See section (1).

Difficulties   There are several long rapids in this section which require scouting, particularly at levels even slightly above normal, especially in the area of Devil's Looking Glass, about 3.5 mi. below the put in. High standing waves will be found on most of these, so following the rule of staying toward the inside of the bend will generally give the safer passage.

Scout the first rapid, located .5 mi. downstream from Tenn. 81 bridge at Embreeville, on the left bank. The main chute is obvious but difficult.

Directions   **Take Out**—Tenn. 67 and 81 bridge. The trip can be shortened some 2 mi. by taking out on the river, left just off Dr. A. J. Willis Rd. The sandy area at this take out is slightly over .5 mi. below the old bridge abutments. Take the first right going west on 81 in Embreeville and proceed approximately 1.4 mi. to this spot.

North Toe River and Toe River

The North Toe heads up east of Minneapolis in the vicinity of Newland. It moves south through a mountainous area until it turns west entering the Toe Valley, which is widely known for its mineral deposits. Below the junction with the South Toe, the river gets considerably wider and becomes known as the Toe. From the Toe's confluence with the Cane the Nolichucky is born.

There are several areas of outstanding scenic beauty, in particular the rock formations of section (3). Unfortunately much of the natural beauty is marred by the grayish color of the water from Spruce Pine down the rest of the river. This is the result of many mica mines and feldspar plants in the area. Although the quality of the water is rather poor, it has improved considerably.

Topo Maps   Newland, Carvers Gap, Spruce Pine, Linville Falls, Micaville, Bakersville, Burnsville, Huntdale

Counties   Avery, Mitchell, Yancey

(1)   Avery Co. Rt. 1164 bridge at Minneapolis to dam at Plumtree

Drop	Difficulty	Distance	Time	Scenery	Water Quality
302'	2-3	8.5 mi.	4 hrs.	B	Good

Gage   U.S. 19E bridge on the southwest side (north of Spruce Pine). Minimum level for solo is the bottom of "1." The upper section can be run only following rain. Sections (2) and (3) can be run year round except following long dry seasons, while the remainder can be run year round.

Difficulties   This section, runnable only with a good runoff, drops continuously over many small stubble fields. Watch for low water bridges and logs. Take out and carry on the left of the dam at Plumtree (15 ft. high), which is located just below the bridge.

(2)   Rt. 1123 south of Spear to U.S. 19E bridge

Drop	Difficulty	Distance	Time	Scenery	Water Quality
102'	1-2	4.5 mi.	2 hrs.	A-B	Good

Gage   3" below "0."

North Toe River and Toe River

Difficulties If starting here, put in about 400 yds. below the dam on Rt. 1123. There is one broken dam a little over halfway down that should be approached and scouted very carefully. This can be run on the left at a good water level. Difficulty class 3+.

(3) U.S. 19E bridge north of Ingalls to U.S. 19E bridge south of Ingalls

Drop	Difficulty	Distance	Time	Scenery	Water Quality
123'	1-2	7.5 mi.	4 hrs.	AA-A	Good to Fair

Gage 6" below "0."

Difficulties Many gravel bars and one ledge that will require some tight turning in approaching it. Can be scouted on the left, run on the right. This is a most scenic area with many overhanging rocks.

(4) U.S. 19E bridge south of Ingalls in Avery Co. to Stroupe Rd.

Drop	Difficulty	Distance	Time	Scenery	Water Quality
123'	1-2	11 mi.	4.5 hrs.	A-B-C	Fair

Gage 6" below "0."

Difficulties Watch closely for a broken dam (10 ft. high) approaching the outskirts of Spruce Pine. The river bends to the left and the paddler should stay to the left, inside the bend, where the carry should be made. This can be a very dangerous area with high water, so proceed with caution. This is a scenic run with many high bluffs over the river.

(5) Stroupe Rd., above the sewage treatment plant in Spruce Pine, to N.C. 80 bridge

Drop	Difficulty	Distance	Time	Scenery	Water Quality
68'	1-2/3	7.5 mi.	3.5 hrs.	B	Fair

Gage 6" below "0."

Difficulties A broken dam about 3 ft. high should be scouted on the right. This may be run on the far left depending on the water level. If doubtful about making it, don't try it! This is located about a mile below the put in. There are two other low washed dams that can be easily scouted.

North Toe River
and Toe River

(6) N.C. 80 bridge at Boonfield in Mitchell Co. to N.C. 197 bridge

Drop	Difficulty	Distance	Time	Scenery	Water Quality
202'	2-3	11.5 mi.	5.5. hrs.	A-B-C	Fair

Gage N.C. 197 bridge, on the southwest side. Minimum level for solo is 5" below "0."

Difficulties 1.5 mi. below the confluence of the South Toe, a class 3, consisting of a boulder garden, should be scouted on the left. Enter on the right. Several canoes have broken up here. Below the bridge at Toecane the river begins dropping faster, at the rate of 30 ft./mi., through a gorge that presents constant white water for close to two miles. The first ledge below the bridge should be scouted.

(7) N.C. 197 bridge south of Red Hill in Mitchell Co. to Yancey Co. Rt. 1338 bridge

Drop	Difficulty	Distance	Time	Scenery	Water Quality
102'	1-2	7.2 mi.	3.5 hrs.	B	Fair

Gage 6" below "0."

Difficulties None; fairly flat, but wider and fast moving.

(8) Yancey Co. Rt. 1338 bridge at Relief to Mitchell Co. Rt. 1321 at Poplar

Drop	Difficulty	Distance	Time	Scenery	Water Quality
100'	1-2	7.6 mi.	3 hrs.	A-B	Fair

Gage 6" below "0."

Difficulties None. A series of shoals occur in the latter portion of this section, beginning 1.5 mi. above Poplar.

Directions **Put In**—Avery Co. Rt. 1164, off U.S. 19E south of Minneapolis. **Take Out**—From N.C. 197 and 226 at Red Hill, go west on Mitchell Co. Rt. 1304 to Rt. 1321, then north to the community of Poplar. Take out across the railroad tracks in front of Molly's Country Store.

North Toe River and Toe River

South Toe River

The South Toe has its headwaters on Mt. Mitchell, the highest peak east of the Rockies (elevation 6,684 ft.), which is south from the put in. It is a delightful stream winding through the mountains over gravel bars and through boulder gardens. Section (2) flows through a particularly scenic area. The water quality drops considerably around Newdale downstream, due to silt from mica mines in the area. It confluences with the North Toe below Newdale to form the Toe River.

Topo Maps   Celo, Micaville

County   Yancey

(1)   Carolina Hemlocks Campground or N.C. 80 bridge north of the campground to Rt. 1152 bridge

Drop	Difficulty	Distance	Time	Scenery	Water Quality
130′	1-2	8 mi.	3.5 hrs.	A-B	Excellent

Gage   U.S.G.S. located 100 yds. above Rt. 1170 bridge on the east bank. Minimum level for solo is 1.09. Can generally be run following periods of wet weather.

Difficulties   Requires a good bit of maneuvering through the gravel bars and over small shoals.

(2)   Rt. 1152 bridge (Bluestone Rd) to N.C. 80 bridge

Drop	Difficulty	Distance	Time	Scenery	Water Quality
108′	1-2-3	6.5 mi.	3.5 hrs.	A	Excellent

Gage   Minimum level for solo is 1.10.

Difficulties   This section cuts through a narrow rocky gorge that has some ledges which will require scouting. The first one has a large flat rock on the left. The second and largest entering the gorge has a series of three drops totaling some 10 ft. in 40 yds. Scout it on the left.

(3)   N.C. 80 bridge in Newdale to Yancey Co. Rt. 1311 on the Toe

Drop	Difficulty	Distance	Time	Scenery	Water Quality
120′	1-2	8 mi.	3.5 hrs.	B	Fair to Poor

Gage Minimum level for solo is .80.

Difficulties None. A lot of maneuvering will be required at low water levels.

Directions **Put In**—N.C. 80 south of U.S. 19E to U.S. Forest Service camp-ground at Carolina Hemlocks.
Take Out—Yancey Co. Rt. 1308 (.5 mi. east of Micaville) north from U.S. 19E for approximately 5.4 mi., then east on Rt. 1311 until reaching the river opposite Lunday. You must ford the creek three times before reaching the river. The take out can be recognized from the river by the footbridge just upstream.

■

Perhaps our grandsons, having never seen a wild river, will never miss the chance to set a canoe in singing water.   Aldo Leopold

South Yadkin River

South Yadkin River

The South Yadkin heads up on the southern slopes of the Brushy Mountains. It flows by Rocky Face (elevation 1,814 ft.), the last prominent peak of the Brushy chain, and heads south and east across the Piedmont to join the Yadkin. We pick it up, just southeast of Rocky Face, as it makes its last drop into the more gently rolling hills of the upper plateau.

Sections (6)-(9) provide some 42 miles of waters suitable for canoe camping.

Note: As streams cut their way through the softer hills of the Piedmont, one will encounter more downed trees, a result of the eroding banks. This becomes the most common difficulty encountered below section (1) and should not be taken lightly—especially at the higher water levels.

Topo Maps   Hiddenite, Central, Harmony, Calahaln, Cool Springs, Coolemee, Churchland

Counties   Alexander, Iredell, Davie, Rowan

(1)   Alexander Co. Rt. 1461 bridge to Alexander Co. Rt. 1456 bridge

Drop	Difficulty	Distance	Time	Scenery	Water Quality
118'	1-2	5 mi.	3.5 hrs.	A	Good

Gage   On Rt. 1461 bridge on the southeast corner. Reading of 6" below "0" is the minimum for a solo run.

Difficulties   A 12 ft. combination dam and ledge is located about 50 yds. down from the put in. Carry on the right. About 1 mi. down, a large tree blocks the only chute. Approach it carefully. About .5 mile beyond the culvert under Rt. 1491, there is an 8 ft. ledge, which possibly could be run off center, angling to the right. Further down, there is a 3 ft. ledge. Carry on the left.

(2)   Alexander Co. Rt. 1456 bridge to Iredell Co. Rt. 1561 bridge

Drop	Difficulty	Distance	Time	Scenery	Water Quality
53'	1	6.8 mi.	2.75 hrs.	A	Good to Fair

Gage   On Iredell Co. Rt. 1570 on the southeast corner. Reading of 6" below "0" is minimum for solo.

South Yadkin River

Difficulties   Water intake unit just below the put in should be approached cautiously. This is at the lower end of Col. R. L. Tatum Water Plant. At slightly higher than normal levels, there are a number of downed trees that could be dangerous.

(3)   Iredell Co. Rt. 1561 bridge to N.C. 115 bridge

Drop	Difficulty	Distance	Time	Scenery	Water Quality
29'	1	4.9 mi.	3 hrs.	B	Fair

Gage   6" below "0" for minimum.

Difficulties   Many downed trees that must be hauled over. A partially washed-out dam is about 4 mi. downstream, that might look tempting. Don't be misled, as there are steel reinforcing rods at the bottom of the chute. Carry it on the right. A drive across the bridge above the dam looks as if it would prove as hairy as trying the chute.

(4)   N.C. 115 bridge to Iredell Co. Rt. 1892 bridge

Drop	Difficulty	Distance	Time	Scenery	Water Quality
19'	C	4.5 mi.	1.5 hrs.	B	Fair

Gage   6" below "0." The river from this point downstream would very seldom be too low to run, other than during an extremely dry spell.

Difficulties   A few downed trees. An 8 ft. slanting dam just above the 1892 bridge. Easy take out or carry on the right, above the water treatment plant. This is one that might lure the neophyte into putting a little excitement into his life. If so, the very heavy hydraulic below won't allow him the opportunity to tell about it.

(5)   Iredell Co. Rt. 1892 bridge to Rt. 2156 bridge

Drop	Difficulty	Distance	Time	Scenery	Water Quality
19'	C	7 mi.	2.5 hrs.	A-B	Fair

Gage   See section (4).

Difficulties   Heavily clogged up below the US 21 bridge for a short distance.

South Yadkin River

(6) Iredell Co. Rt. 2156 bridge to the side of Rt. 2145 (beneath the I-40 bridge)

Drop	Difficulty	Distance	Time	Scenery	Water Quality
28′	C	11.3 mi.	3.5 hrs.	A-B	Fair

Gage   See section (4)

Difficulties   None. Perhaps an occasional downed tree.

(7) Iredell Co. Rt. 2145 (beneath I-40 bridge) to Davie Co. Rt. 1143 bridge

Drop	Difficulty	Distance	Time	Scenery	Water Quality
21′	C	9.2 mi.	3 hrs.	A-B	Fair

Gage   See section (4)

Difficulties   Watch for possible downed trees.

(8) Davie Co. Rt. 1143 bridge to US 601 bridge

Drop	Difficulty	Distance	Time	Scenery	Water Quality
34′	-1/2	11.7 mi.	3.75 hrs.	A-B	Fair

Gage   See section (4)

Difficulties   Dam at Coolemee (7 mi. below the put in). Approach it on the
right carefully. Take out is about 30 yds. above the dam in a low
open area. A well defined trail leads around the dam, a carry of about 100
yds. A class 2 chute in the center below is runnable by approaching it from the
right.
    For those who don't wish to run the 2.5 mi. of slack water above the dam, a
take out can be made at a ramp at Bear Creek, off Davie Co. Rt. 1116.

(9) US 601 bridge to N.C. 150 bridge over the Yadkin River

Drop	Difficuilty	Distance	Time	Scenery	Water Quality
5′	C	9.9 mi.	3 hrs.	A-B	Fair

Gage   See section (4)

154

Difficulties   None, other than maneuvering around an occasional downed tree.

Directions   **Put In**—North on Alexander Co. Rt. 1001 off N.C. 90 in Hiddenite, then east on Alexander Co. Rt. 1461.
Take Out—N.C. 150 north of Salisbury.

Upper Creek

Upper Creek flows out of the Pisgah National Forest, which helps to provide the clear water that makes it a fine trout stream and reportedly one of the best small mouth bass fishing streams in the southeast. It is a small clear stream flowing primarly through gravel bars and small riffles.

Topo Maps   Oak Hill, Morganton North

County   Burke

(1) Rt. 1405 bridge (Adako Rd.) to Rt. 1439 bridge

Drop	Difficulty	Distance	Time	Scenery	Water Quality
25'	1/2	4.5 mi.	2 hrs.	B	Good

Gage   Located on the southwest piling of Rt. 1405 bridge. Minimum for solo is 6'' below "0."

Difficulties   One ledge about .5 mi. below the put in. Watch for downed trees throughout all sections.

(2) Rt. 1439 bridge at Worry (Henderson Mill Rd.) to Rt. 1440 bridge

Drop	Difficulty	Distance	Time	Scenery	Water Quality
21'	1/2	3.5 mi.	1.5 hrs.	B	Good

Gage   Located on a concrete slab under Rt. 1439 bridge on the east side. Minimum for solo is 7'' below "0."

Difficulties   One fast narrow chute about halfway down the section. Watch for downed trees.

(3) Rt. 1440 bridge (Bost Rd.) to N.C. 18 bridge on the Catawba River

Drop	Difficulty	Distance	Time	Scenery	Water Quality
Flat	1	3.5 mi.	1.5 hrs.	C	Good

Gage   Minimum for solo is 7'' below "0."

Difficulties   None

Directions   **Put In**—East on Rt. 1405 off N.C. 181 northwest of Morganton.
Take Out—N.C. 18 bridge over the Catawba River north of
Morganton. The bridge is immediately below the confluence of
Upper Creek with the Catawba.

Uwharrie River

The Uwharrie heads up west of Asheboro and flows generally south through the Uwharrie Mountains and across portions of the Uwharrie National Forest before it flows into Lake Tillery. The river meanders greatly through small floodplains and steep valley walls, which present some very scenic bluffs. The bed is primarily one of long pools with occasional ripples.

The area is widely known for its gold mining activity. North Carolina's first deep gold mines were found in Montgomery County in the early 1820s. In fact, several mines were worked along the river itself late in the nineteenth century. The largest of these was the Coggins Mine, just up Rt. 1301, west of the river. This was the most important mine in the state from 1915 until the late 1920s. The paddler may want to bring along a pan and take a longer than usual lunch break. It may pay for the gas to run the shuttle—one way, that is!

Note to hikers: A hiking trail, referred to as GUMPAC, has been developed in a corridor along the ridges paralleling the river. The trail, developed primarily through the efforts of a group of private citizens (Greater Uwharrie Mountains Preservation and Appreciation Committee) will hopefully be included soon as a component of the State Trails System.

Topo Maps   Asheboro, Albemarle

Counties   Randolph, Montgomery

(1)   N.C. 49 bridge to Randolph Co. Rt. 1143 bridge

Drop	Difficulty	Distance	Time	Scenery	Water Quality
22′	C-1	11.5 mi.	4 hrs.	A-B	Fair

Gage   U.S.G.S. gage 100 yds. downstream from N.C. 109 on the north bank. Minimum for solo is 1.6. Runnable year round except during extremely long dry periods.

Difficulties   Watch for an occasional downed tree. A 5 ft. dam located just above Rt. 1143 bridge can be carried fairly easily on the left side. Approach cautiously at higher water levels. Some two miles of back water will be found above it.

(2)   Randolph Co. Rt. 1143 bridge to Montgomery Co. Rt. 1301 bridge

Drop	Difficulty	Distance	Time	Scenery	Water Quality
24′	1-2	7.7 mi.	2.75 hrs.	A	Fair

Uwharrie River

wharrie River

Gage   See section (1)

Difficulties   None.

(3)   Montgomery Co. Rt. 1301 bridge to side of Forest Service Rd. 555 (Cotton Place Rd.), 2.9 mi. below N.C. 109 bridge

Drop	Difficulty	Distance	Time	Scenery	Water Quality
46'	1-2	10.6 mi.	4.5 hrs.	A	Fair

Gage   See section (1)

Difficulties   None.

(4)   Forest Service Rd. 555 to Morrow Mountain State Park, directly across Lake Tillery from the mouth of the Uwharrie

Drop	Difficulty	Distance	Time	Scenery	Water Quality
23'	1-2	6.6 mi.	2.75 hrs.	A	Fair

Gage   See section (1)

Difficulties   None.

Directions   **Put In**—N.C. 49 bridge east of Asheboro.
Take Out—Morrow Mountain State Park, off of N.C. 740, northeast of Albemarle. For those who wish to extend the trip some 6 mi. down the lake, a boat launching ramp is located on the east side below N.C. 24-27-73 bridge, southeast of Troy.

Watauga River

The Watauga heads up on the western slopes of Grandfather Mountain, then winds its way along N.C. 105 until it cuts west. After leaving 105 it meanders through hilly pasture lands on the way to the spectacularly rugged Watauga Gorge before reaching Watauga Lake in Tennessee.

Section (2) is a very pleasant, easy float trip for anyone, while section (4) is anything but that. It is not by any stretch of the imagination a run for open boats, but with no known published information on the gorge, it was decided to include it for its reference value for decked boaters. The gorge has several falls and many huge boulders that make it a run for advanced paddlers only.

Information on section (4) is taken from notes of Ed Gertler and David Benner.

Section (5), after its emergence from a deep gorge below Wilbur Dam, moves on through more pastoral country. Sycamore Shoals, just above the take out, is where the Over Mountain Men began their historic march to Kings Mountain.

Topo Maps   Boone, Valle Crucis, Sherwood (N.C.); Elk Mills, Watauga Dam, Elizabethton (Tenn.)

Counties   Watauga (N.C.); Johnson (Tenn.)

(1)   N.C. 105 bridge to N.C. 194 bridge at Valle Crucis

Drop	Difficulty	Distance	Time	Scenery	Water Quality
175'	1-2	4.5 mi.	2 hrs.	A-B	Good

Gage   U.S.G.S. gage is on the right bank 250 ft. upstream from Rt. 1121 bridge. Minimum reading for solo is 1.95. The river can be run throughout most of the year below section (1), except during long dry periods.

Difficulties   This section runs over a bed of rocks with some small ledges that can require a lot of maneuvering.

(2)   N.C. 194 bridge to U.S. 321 bridge

Drop	Difficulty	Distance	Time	Scenery	Water Quality
65'	1-2	7.5 mi.	2.5 hrs.	B	Good

Watauga River

Gage   U.S.G.S. minimum for solo is 1.85.

Difficulties   One low water bridge. Below Rt. 1121 bridge there is a 15 ft.
                   dam that can be portaged on the right (50 yds.). A few gravel
bars other than these.

(3)   U.S. 321 bridge to Watauga Co. Rt. 1200 (Guys Ford Rd.)

Drop	Difficulty	Distance	Time	Scenery	Water Quality
100'	2/3	4 mi.	2 hrs.	A	Good

Gage   U.S.G.S. gage. Minimum for solo is 1.85.

Difficulties   There is a drop of some 12 ft. within 20 yds. about .25 mi.
                   below the put in. This can be seen from the highway. It can be
run 2/3 of the way down, but the bottom is packed with boulders. A carry can
be made on the right. Other than this, it is primarily a run through gravel bars
and small boulder fields.

(4)   Watauga Rt. 1200 (Guys Ford Bridge) to Watauga Lake

Drop	Difficulty	Distance	Time	Scenery	Water Quality
515'*	3-4-5/6	5.7 mi.	5 hrs.	A-A	Good

* 3 parts drop at the rate of 200'/mi. for approximately .2 mile each.

Gage   U.S.G.S. gage. Minimum for solo is 1.85, or 21" below top of
                  center piling on downstream side of Guys Ford Bridge. An esti-
mated maximum level is 10" below the top of the piling.

Difficulties   The gorge starts off with easy boulder rapids and small ledges
                   before reaching a short, steep clogged rapid where it turns hard
right and the bottom falls out. Beyond the first rapid, which is quite clogged,
there follow two drops that definitely should be scouted and might be run,
depending on the water level.
   The river for some distance is a succession of boulder piles, natural dams,
and individual drops up to 6 ft. high, which can be run. Primarily the bed is
filled with boulders which block the downstream view almost constantly.
   Two exceptions to the above are straightways bearing to the left where the
river runs through long rapids with waves and holes, and the view relatively

open. The second stretch, which is approximately 1 mi. below the first, terminates in a 15 ft. falls. The paddler should land at the head of the stretch and scout. Kent Taylor, on his first trip down this section, missed the eddy at the top and went over backwards, no less. Carry it on the left.

From the top of the falls a house-size boulder can be seen. Below it is an 8 ft. vertical ledge which might be run, depending on the water level. Scout it for sure. At this point the geology of the river undergoes a change and what has been a boulder river now becomes a ledge river. The river eases up somewhat for the rest of the run to the lake, but there are still many good rapids.

(5)   Wilbur Dam to .5 mi. west of Sycamore Shoals on U.S. 321

Drop	Difficulty	Distance	Time	Scenery	Water Quality
158'	2-3	11.5 mi.	5.5 hrs.	A-B	Good

Gage   U.S.G.S. gage is on the left bank at 19E (Bristol Highway) bridge. Minimum reading for solo is 2.68. There is no regular schedule for water releases from Wilbur Dam, as power is furnished on demand. The only apparent pattern of release occurs on Saturdays shortly after 12 noon during the summer.

Difficulties   At lower water levels, when the dam isn't operating, there are no dangerous areas, but Sycamore Shoals should be approached with caution. At higher levels the picture changes. About 300 yds. downstream from the overhead foot bridge in the gorge, a series of ledges build up 3-4 ft. standing waves in a bend to the left. If not prepared to handle this, stay close to the left bank.

Downstream from 19E bridge the Beaunit Plant on the left and the Elizabethton sewage palnt on the right of the river dump waste into the river, which gives one added motivation to stay upright through Sycamore Shoals. It can be recognized by a long flat stretch and the fort on the left side. The shoals can best be scouted from the left. It consists of a series of ledges on the right, running diagonally downstream from right to left. The safest passage is to the right of the main channel.

Directions   **Put In**—N.C. 105 bridge south of Boone.

Take Out—**Section (4)** Go north off U.S. 321 (approximately 2 mi. east of the Elk River bridge) on the road to Gregg Boat Dock and bear right along the lake shore as far as possible.

Put In—Section (5) Take Tenn. 91 north from Elizabethton to the community of Hunter (alongside river) and take the first main road to the right after 91 leaves the river. Proceed approximately 4 mi. to the dam.

Take Out—Go west on U.S. 321 from Elizabethton approximately .5 mi. beyond Sycamore Shoals Historical Area.

Watauga River

Wilson Creek

Wilson Creek

Wilson Creek has its headwaters on the eatern slopes of Grandfather Mountain. With its watershed primarily within the Pisgah National Forest, it has exceptional water quality. This quality quite often fools even the experienced paddler into underestimating water depth.

The upper stretch runs through rock gardens and over an occasional ledge before it starts the fast descent through the ruggedly beautiful gorge with its large boulders and small falls. After leaving the gorge at Brown Mountain Beach it reverts back to the characteristics of the upper section. Fortunately, the gorge, as well as most of the creek, can be enjoyed by everyone and not only those who have the skill to paddle it. Wilson Gorge is highly recommended to all—whether paddling or driving. One should be aware that the creek, especially through the gorge, has become a very popular area. The traffic on the narrow road is very heavy on weekends from late spring through the summer.

Topo Maps   Chestnut Mtn., Colletteville

County   Caldwell

(1)   Rt. 1328 concrete low water bridge to point 150 yds. south of National Forest boundary sign

Drop	Difficulty	Distance	Time	Scenery	Water Quality
120'	2-3	5 mi.	2.5 hrs.	A-B	Excellent

Gage   Located on the south side of the center piling on Rt. 1337 (Adako Rd.) bridge. Minimum for solo is 6" below "0." Water level stays good all year round, except during long dry spells.

Difficulties   Most of sections (1) and (2) can be scouted from the road.

About .5 mi. below the put in, as the creek bends to the right, there is a low foot bridge that can be missed by a quick move to the left.

Lunch Stop Rapid, a Class 3, narrows down, piling the water against it and forcing it to the left of a rock wall. This should be scouted on the left and run on the inside. The rock makes for an excellent stopping place for lunch.

There are several ledges and stubble fields below the steel bridge that may require scouting depending on the water levels. Be sure that the take out is checked out and that it can be easily recognized, or the gorge may see you before you see the gorge.

168

(2)   Approximately 400 yds. south of the boundary sign, below 10 ft. falls to wherever one decides that enough is enough.

Drop	Difficulty	Distance	Time	Scenery	Water Quality
220'	3-4-5	2.4 mi.	5 hrs.	A	Excellent

Gage   Minimum for solo is 4" below "0." Maximum is 1" below "0."

Difficulties   The stretch for some 250 yds. between the take out on section (1) and the put in on section (2) contains rapids in the high Class 5 area and ends with a 10 ft. falls, thus the reason for excluding it.

This section, although quite short, will require a great deal of scouting. Generally, most of the drops are followed by pools where one can recover or empty one's boat. There are four rapids in this section that require carrying and depending on the paddler's skill, there will possibly be others.

The gorge is not a run to be taken lightly. It is a favorite place for tubing, although it has claimed one or two tuber's lives each year for the past several years.

(3)   200 yds. above Rt. 1337 bridge on Rt. 1328 to Burke Co. Rt. 1438 bridge over the Johns River

Drop	Difficulty	Distance	Time	Scenery	Water Quality
42'	1-2	8 mi.	3.5 hrs.	B-C	Good

Gage   Minimum for solo is 6" below "0."

Difficulties   There is one rapid, "Eddie's Icebox," approaching Class 3 in difficulty, about .5 mi. below Adako bridge, which requires a hard right turn. It will carry the unwary paddler directly onto the rock ledge straight in front. Step out on the small island to the left to scout.

One other rapid between Perkins Park and Playmore Beach can be trouble at lower water levels. Most of the water runs off a ledge on the far right, which is where it should be run.

Directions   **Put In**—Caldwell Co. Rt. 1328 north of Rt. 1337 1 mi. northeast of Burke-Caldwell Co. line. Low water bridge is .6 mi. south of Mortimer.
Take Out—West on Rt. 1337 (Burke Co. Rt. 1405) 2.2. mi. from Wilson Creek bridge, to Burke Co. Rt. 1424 (Grade Rt.). Go south on it to Rt. 1438, then east to Corpening Bridge.

Section 4

Dan River

The Dan flows off the crest of the Blue Ridge beneath the Pinnacles of Dan, where it is piped down the mountain through the turbines of the city of Danville Power Plant, above the community of Kibler. From the Power Plant until it reaches the town of Danbury, it wanders through hills covered with laurel and rhododendron. As one paddles the North Carolina sections, he will catch glimpses of the Sauratown Mountains to the south, one of the most easterly mountainous areas in the state, where Hanging Rock State Park is located. The park consists of rugged mountain terrain and has excellent camping facilities.

Sections (3), (4), and (5) of the Dan are outstanding for the novice fast water paddler who seeks further experience. The author spent many happy times paddling and exploring the Dan with Tom Lowe of Winston-Salem during our early paddling days. It is still pleasant to recall coming around a bend and sighting Pilot Mountain looming above in the distance.

Topo Maps   Claudville, Stuart S.E.(Va.); Hanging Rock, Danbury (N.C.)

Counties   Patrick (Va.); Stokes (N.C.)

(1)   City of Danville Power Plant at Kibler to Patrick Co. Rt. 773 bridge

Drop	Difficulty	Distance	Time	Scenery	Water Quality
255' 1 mi. @ 65'/mi.	1-2-3	8 mi.	3.5 hrs.	B	Excellent

Gage   None. To check on the water flow, call Pinnacles Hydroelectric Station, (703) 251-5141 and ask for the water flow. 5,600 k.w. would be a minimum. Maximum possible flow is 9,600, at which open canoes can run safely.

Difficulties   The first .5 mile below the put in drops very fast. About 200 yds. below the first bridge, a 3 ft. drop pushes much of the water into a large boulder on the right. If entered too far to the right, much of the boat is also pushed against the boulder. This rock is undercut, so be very cautious in trying to dislodge a broached canoe.

A very low water bridge is located around a bend to the right, about 2 mi. below the power plant. Stay close to the right.

Dan River

(2)   Patrick Co. Rt. 773 bridge to Stokes Co. Rt. 1432

Drop	Difficulty	Distance	Time	Scenery	Water Quality
224'	1-2/3	12.5 mi.	5.5 hrs.	A	Good

Gage   U.S.G.S. gage located 75' above N.C. 704 bridge on the north
                bank. A reading of 1.7 is minimum for solo, or phone Pinnacles
for a reading (5,600 k.w. minimum).

Difficulties   Primarily fast water approaches through small rock gardens and
                over small ledges.
    Following the second bridge (Stokes Co. Rt. 1416) below Va. 103 bridge,
there is a series of ledges ending in a Class III, requiring an "S" turn. Scout on
the left. Stokes Co. Rt. 1417 (Joyce Mill Rd.) is immediately below these rapids.

(3)   Stokes Co. Rt. 1432 bridge (Collinstown Rd.) at Jessups Mill to
N.C. 704 bridge

Drop	Difficulty	Distance	Time	Scenery	Water Quality
128'	1-2	8.5 mi.	4 hrs.	A	Good

Gage   U.S.G.S. is 1.7 minimum for solo.

Difficulties   One rapid where the river drops abruptly over a bed of rocks
                and narrows down between two large boulders. Easily recog-
nizable. An excellent lunch stop.

(4)   N.C. 704 bridge to N.C. 89 bridge

Drop	Difficulty	Distance	Time	Scenery	Water Quality
72'	1-2	7 mi.	3 hrs.	A	Good

Gage   U.S.G.S. gage is 1.55 minimum for solo.

Difficulties   Many small gravel bars at lower water levels.

(5)   N.C. 89 bridge (Clements Ford) to Rt. 1674 bridge at Danbury

Drop	Difficulty	Distance	Time	Scenery	Water Quality
70'	1-2	10.5 mi.	5 hrs.	A-B	Good

Gage   U.S.G.S. gage is 1.55 minimum for solo.

Difficulties   None, other than one sharply undercut bank in a sharp bend to the left, just below the put in. Below the second bridge after N.C. 89 be on the lookout for some caves in the cliff on the right. The more ambitious may be tempted to climb to them. The difficulty here is the great clusters of poison ivy growing in the entrance.

Directions   **Put In**—Va. Rt. 103 northeast of Mt. Airy, N.C., to Patrick Co. Rt. 773, northeast to Rt. 648, then north to the end of road at city of Danville Power Plant.

Ask permission at the plant to launch below. There is not much parking space in the immediate area, so be very careful not to block driveways in any way.

Take Out—On the sandbar on the right, 100 yds. above Stokes Co. Rt. 1674 bridge at Danbury, and east of N.C. 89.

■

I went to the woods because I wished to live deliberately, to front only the essential facts of life, and see if I could not learn what it had to teach, and not, when I came to die, discover that I had not lived.

                                                              Thoreau

Elk Creek

Elk Creek cuts through the deep valley below Elk Ridge on its way to join the Yadkin River just below Elkville. It is a small, fast moving stream meandering through farm lands before making a last dash, dropping through a beautiful gorge above Elkville.

Topo Map   Grandin

County   Wilkes

(1)   Rt. 1162 above Darby to N.C. 268 bridge

Drop	Difficulty	Distance	Time	Scenery	Water Quality
194'	2-3	8.4 mi.	4 hrs.	A-B	Good

Gage   U.S.G.S. gage is located 100 ft. above the last ledge on stream, above 268 bridge on the east bank. Minimum reading for solo paddling is 1.15. This is a low water stream which can be run in the spring and during or following rains.

Difficulties   Many small pebble fields and rock gardens. The last 600 yds. through the gorge drops rather fast over ledges that will require a lot of maneuvering. Much of the gorge can be scouted from Rt. 1162 when the foliage isn't too thick. With higher water levels (above 1.55), scouting closely will become a necessity.

Directions   **Put In**—Wilkes Co. Rt. 1162 off N.C. 268 at Elkville, to where the road touches the river just above the community of Darby. At low water levels, put in can be made 4.3 mi. above N.C. 268 alongside the road. This cuts the trip almost in half.

Take Out—Below the last ledge, about 100 yds. above N.C. 268 bridge, on the east bank. This is private property; ask permission at the building above.

Fisher River

The author feels the Fisher is the ideal stream for the novice to begin his fast water paddling. It presents no really difficult rapids, primarily small riffles, but does require one to maneuver the craft and read the water well. The banks are pretty with many hillsides solid with rhododendron and for the most part there is little evidence of habitation. In the spring the Fisher appears to team with wildlife. For a nice leisurely paddle, try the Fisher.

Topo Maps   Dobson, Copeland

County   Surry

(1)   Old U.S. 601 bridge to N.C. 268 bridge

Drop	Difficulty	Distance	Time	Scenery	Water Quality
86'	1-2	8.5 mi.	4 hrs.	A-B	Good

Gage   U.S.G.S. gage is at the N.C. 268 bridge, 500 ft. upstream on the east bank. Minimum level for solo run is 2.20.

Difficulties   Shallows and pebble fields.

(2)   N.C. 268 bridge to the community of Rockford, on the Yadkin River

Drop	Difficulty	Distance	Time	Scenery	Water Quality
78'	1-2	11.5 mi.	5 hrs.	A-B	Good

Difficulties   Shallows and pebble fields, except for a washed-out dam just below the put in, which should be approached cautiously. A Class 2 located between the second and third bridges can be recognized by the large flat rock blocking most of the stream. Best passage at lower levels is on the far left. At 2.90 or above, the right side of the left channel can be run. If one looks closely one will find the large rock is pock-marked with garnets.

Watch out for the low water bridge at higher water levels after entering the Yadkin.

A slightly shorter run can be made by combining the last part of section (1) and the major part of section (2). Put in at Rt. 1100 bridge, and take out at Rt. 2233 bridge (approximately 8 mi.)

Direcitons **Put In**—Old U.S. 601 bridge northeast of Dobson.
Take Out—Surry Co. Rt. 2221 south, off N.C. 268 (.3 mi. west of the 268 bridge) to Rockford Community Park, .3 mi. south of Rockford. This will be 200 yds. downstream from Yadkin Co. 1510 low water bridge on the north bank. If Yadkin is high, take out on the north bank just above the low water bridge.

178

Lewis Fork, North Prong

The North Prong of the Lewis Fork heads up on the slopes of the Blue Ridge, and winds its way through the valley between Yates Mountain on the south and Judd Mountain on the north, before joining the South Prong and running on into Kerr Scott impoundment. The stream is primarily one of ledges, presenting a natural slalom course in several stretches. Most of the run is through a secluded area, until the last mile or so, where it becomes more pastoral.

Topo Map   Purlear

County   Wilkes

(1)   Wilkes Co. Rt. 1304 bridge to Rt. 1307, just below the confluence of the South Prong

Drop	Difficulty	Distance	Time	Scenery	Water Quality
141' .6 mi. @ 66'/mi.	2-3	4.2 mi.	2.5 hrs.	A	Good

Gage   On the east side of Rt. 1304 bridge, at the put in. Minimum for solo is a reading of 5" below the "0." Generally runnable during wet seasons. A reading of 1" or 2" above the bottom of the "0" is probably maximum.

Difficulties   About 10 yds. below the first ledge, extending across the entire river bed, are two strands of barbed wire. The first can be raised and the second can be paddled over at a decent water level.
  In the second mile, just beyond a bend to the right, there is a drop of some 20' within 80 yds. This stretch can best be scouted from the left.
  A few hundred feet above the take out, a large tree blocks the passage at Rt. 1311 bridge. This can become a dangerous spot at higher water levels. At lower levels a boat can be worked around on the left side.

Directions   **Put In**—Go west on U.S. 421 approximately 8 mi from Wilkesboro, to Rt. 1307 (just beyond the 421 bridge over the Lewis Fork), then north to Rt. 1304 and right for approximately 1 mi. to the 1304 bridge. There is limited parking area, so be careful not to park in yards.
  Take Out—(See put in.) The take out is a couple of hundred yards north of U.S. 421 on Rt. 1307.

A run of an additional 4 mi. can be made by extending the trip down the Lewis Fork into Kerr Scott Lake, and taking out at Smithey's Creek Public Use Area. This can be reached by going east 1 mi. from Rt. 1307 on U.S. 421, to Rt. 1145 and then south.

Lewis Fork, North Prong
Lewis Fork, South Prong

Lewis Fork, South Prong

The South Prong of the Lewis Fork runs along U.S. 421 between Dividing Ridge and Yates Mountain, to join the North Prong before entering Kerr Scott Lake. The run here is primarily over small gravel bars interspersed with an occasional ledge, through a fairly remote wooded area.

Topo Map   Purlear

County   Wilkes

(1)   Wilkes Co. Rt. 1156 bridge to Rt. 1307, just below the confluence of the North Prong

Drop	Difficulty	Distance	Time	Scenery	Water Quality
89' .4 mi. @ 50'/mi.	1-2	3.5 mi.	2 hrs.	A	Good

Gage   On the south side of Rt. 1154 bridge. Minimum for solo is a reading of 6" below the "0." Generally runnable during wet seasons.

Difficulties   There is one slanting ledge, easily recognizable, which should be approached rather cautiously at higher water levels. The overall drop throughout the entire run is fairly gradual.

Directions   **Put In**—West on U.S. 421 approximately 9 mi. from Wilkesboro, to Rt. 1154; then northwest to the bridge, left beyond the bridge on Rt. 1305 for .6 mi. to the put in.
   Take Out—See directions for Lewis Fork, North Prong.

Little River

The Little heads up on the slopes of Peach Bottom Mountain and winds its way through the foothills of the Blue Ridge to join the New River in Grayson County, Virginia. The entire run of the river is quite remote and very scenic.

Topo Map   Sparta East

Counties   Alleghany (N.C.); Grayson (Va.)

(1)   Alleghany Rt. 1424 bridge to Rt. 1433 bridge

Drop	Difficulty	Distance	Time	Scenery	Water Quality
147'	1-2/4	7.8 mi.	3.5 hrs.	A	Good

Gage   On the northwest side of Rt. 1424 bridge. Minimum level for solo is 5" below the bottom of "0." Runnable primarily during wet seasons.

Difficulties   Watch for cables and barbed wire below the second bridge (Rt. 1426). About 2 mi. below this bridge, at a point just upstream from where Rt. 1428 comes down to the river on the south side, the river narrows down. About 50 ft. below is a 3.5 ft. ledge, forming a natural dam, followed immediately by a 2 ft. ledge. Carry on the right. At higher levels move right immediately below the narrow chute, since a strong hydraulic is formed below.

Approximately 1 mi. below the confluence of Glade Creek there is a 3 ft. ledge that should be scouted on the far left. Approach it cautiously.

(2)   Alleghany Rt. 1433 bridge to N.C. 18

Drop	Difficulty	Distance	Time	Scenery	Water Quality
53'	1-2	3.4 mi.	1.5 hrs.	A	Good

Gage   Minimum level for solo is 6" below "0."

Difficulties   At slightly higher levels the stretch from below the confluence of Brush Creek down to N.C. 18 can become rather heavy.

(3)   N.C. 18 to Grayson Co. Rt. 632 bridge

Drop	Difficulty	Distance	Time	Scenery	Water Quality
126'	1-2	7.7 mi.	3 hrs.	A	Good

Gage　　　　Minimum level for solo on the gage at Rt. 1424 is 7" below "0."
There is also a roughly painted gage on 18 bridge. Minimum for solo can be judged as the same distance below the bottom of the "0" as the distance between numbers 1 and 2. Measurement between the numbers varies considerably.

Difficulties　　At one point about halfway down this stretch there is a natural weir which funnels most of the water through a rock garden on the inside of a hard bend to the right. It should be approached cautiously.

Directions　　**Put In**—Northeast on N.C. 18 from Sparta for 1.1 mi., to Rt. 1424, then east for 1.1. mi. to the bridge.
Take Out—From N.C. 18, go north on Alleghany Rt. 1414, turn right on 1412, cross the state line, and turn right again on Grayson Rt. 632 to the bridge.

For those who might like to extend the trip on into the New River, there is a run of 15 mi. to U.S. 58-221 bridge west of Galax, Va. There is one low water bridge (Rt. 626) about 1.2 mi. down from Rt. 632.

Mayo River, North Fork

The North Fork of the Mayo flows through heavily woded hills after leaving the pasture lands at the beginning of the section. It has more gradient than the upper reaches of the South Fork, thus providing a more interesting trip. Once it joins the South Fork, the Mayo is formed and it drops over a series of ledges that give the effect of a natural staircase. The latter part of the trip contains some of the best white water available to paddlers in the northern Piedmont and eastern North Carolina. It makes for an excellent training course.

Unfortunately, the runs on the North Fork and the South Fork may be short lived as neighboring cities and counties eye them for sources for increasing water needs.

Topo Map   Price (Va.)

Counties   Henry (Va.); Rockingham (N.C.)

(1)   Henry Co. Rt. 629 bridge to Rockingham Co. Rt. 1359

Drop	Difficulty	Distance	Time	Scenery	Water Quality
56'	2-3	4.2 mi.	2.5 hrs.	B	Good

Gage   U.S.G.S. gage is 400 ft. south of Rt. 629 bridge, on the east bank. Minimum level for solo run is 1.55. Maximum for lower part of section is 2.6.

U.S.G.S. gage is 300 ft. downstream from Rockingham Co. Rt. 1358 bridge, on the west bank. Minimum for solo is 1.38, maximum 2.3. Can be run except during long dry spells.

Difficulties   Two ledges on the upper section might require scouting. Both are recognizable before getting too close. Both can generally be run on the far left.

Below the confluence, the staircase will require a great deal of maneuvering to locate the best passage in low water, and a great deal of care in high water. Below Rt. 1358 bridge, a 3 ft. ledge has a wide open chute on the left. Thirty yds below it, a series of ledges drop some 8 ft. within 15 yds. This is best entered at left center and by angling diagonally right across the current, before dropping through a slot not much wider than a canoe. A hard left turn must be made immediately, in order to miss the rock in the center of the bottom of the passage. The gradient averages 20 ft. per mile through this last mile.

Directions   **Put In**—From Rockingham Co. Rt. 1358 (the extension of Rt. 1381), go north on Rt. 1360 and Henry Co. Rt. 693 (1.1 mi. east of Rt. 1358 bridge) to Henry Co. Rt. 629, west to the bridge. Old homestead northeast of the bridge has a road down it, which leads to the riverside. This is private property. If in doubt, check at the house across the river before entering.

Take Out—Rockingham Rt. 1360, west off U.S. 220 to Rt. 1381; then west to Rt. 1359, which runs down the east side of the river. Go .4 mi. to where Rt. 1385 cuts east.

For an extended trip, one may wish to paddle on down the Mayo to N.C. 770 bridge (distance is 6 mi.; time is 3-3.5 hrs.; class 1). Take N.C. 770 west off U.S. 220 at Stoneville, N.C.

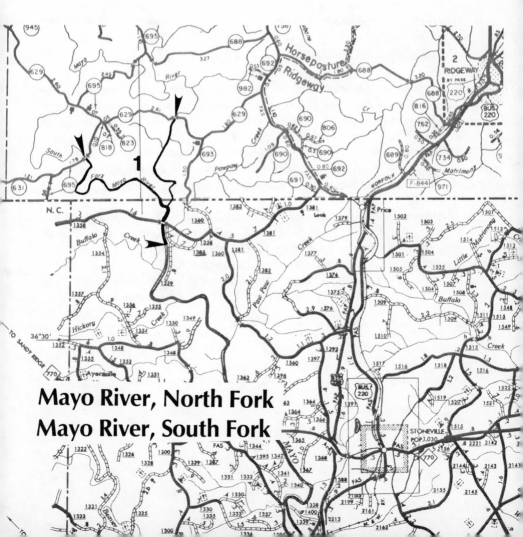

Mayo River, North Fork
Mayo River, South Fork

Mayo River, South Fork

The South Fork of the Mayo meanders through woodlands, presenting the paddler with easy riffles, until it confluences with the North Fork. From there down to the take out the river drops faster over a series of ledges, and gives a more challenging course.

Topo Maps   Spencer, Price (Va.)

Counties   Henry (Va.); Rockingham (N.C.)

(1)   Henry Co. Rt. 695 bridge to Rockingham Co. Rt. 1359

Drop	Difficulty	Distance	Time	Scenery	Water Quality
54′	2-3	5 mi.	3 hrs.	A-B	Good

Gage   U.S.G.S. gage is 300 ft. downstream from Rockingham Co. Rt. 1358 bridge, on the west bank. Minimum level for solo run is 1.38; maximum for lower part of the section is 2.3. Can be run except during long dry spells.

Difficulties   None in the range of levels mentioned as maximum and minimum. Primarily a run of easy riffles. For more information on the area below the confluence, refer to the Mayo River, North Fork.

Directions   **Put In**—Go west on Rockingham Co. Rt. 1358 bridge (Stokes Co. Rt. 1625) to Stokes Co. Rt. 1630, north to Henry Co. Rt. 695, then northeast to the bridge. Rt. 695 can also be reached from Rt. 629 west of North Fork bridge, and then southwest on Rt. 695.

Take Out—Reverse the above directions and refer to the directions for take out on the North Fork of the Mayo.

Angus Morrison running Nantahala Falls in C-1.
Photo courtesy of the Nantahala Outdoor Center.

Mitchell River

Mitchell River

The Mitchell flows off the foothills of the Blue Ridge to join the Yadkin. It is a fast low water stream flowing over small ledges and through rock gardens. The water quality is generally quite clear, while the heavily wooded banks give the impression of complete wilderness. If the water table remained at a high enough level much of the year, this would surely be one of North Carolina's most popular float streams.

Topo Map   Elkin North

County   Surry

(1)   Rt. 1315 bridge to Rt. 1001 bridge

Drop	Difficulty	Distance	Time	Scenery	Water Quality
131'	1-2	6 mi.	3 hrs.	A	Excellent-Good

Gage   U.S.G.S. gage is at Rt. 1001 bridge, 18 ft. upstream on the west bank. A minimum reading of 2.5 is necessary for solo running. Can be run during the spring and after rain.

Difficulties   None, other than fast water running through rock gardens.

(2)   Rt. 1001 bridge to N.C. 268 bridge

Drop	Difficulty	Distance	Time	Scenery	Water Quality
69'	1-2	4.5 mi.	2 hrs.	A	Excellent-Good

Gage   Minimum reading of 2.18 for solo.

Difficulties   Bed is similar to the above, with the exception of one 3 ft. ledge located just above the take out. This can present a hydraulic at higher water levels.

Directions   **Put In**—Surry Co. Rt. 1315 bridge, east off U.S. 21 and 1 mi. east of the town of Mountain Park.
Take Out—N.C. 268 bridge 4.5 mi. east of Elkin city limits, and just above its confluence with the Yadkin River. A run of an additional 4.5 mi. can be made by extending the trip into the Yadkin and taking out at U.S. 601 bridge at Crutchfield.

Reddies River

Reddies River

The Reddies flows out of the Blue Ridge Moutains between Judd Mountain and Burke Mountain to North Wilkesboro, where it joins the Yadkin River. Mostly it flows through forested land interspersed with farm land. The first two miles, with a 20 ft. per mile gradient, is where it's at—the white water, that is— but the entire section, except for the last mile, will give the paddler a pleasant float trip. A dam has been authorized on the lower part of the section, which will impound some 2,056 acres of water, so one may not have much to paddle in the future.

Topo Map   Wilkesboro

County   Wilkes

(1)   Rt. 1546 to city limits of North Wilkesboro

Drop	Difficulty	Distance	Time	Scenery	Water Quality
115'	1-2/3	10 mi.	4.5 hrs.	A-B	Good

Gage   U.S.G.S. is on the east bank 400 ft. upstream from Rt. 1517 bridge. Minimum for solo is 1.30. Can be run throughout most of the year, except during prolonged dry spells.

Difficulties   The Class 3 rapid is in the first mile, where a series of three ledges drop about 12 ft. within 20 yds. Scout on the left and enter on the left. This stretch of 2 mi. from the put in to Rt. 1540, which includes the Class 3, can be run in less than 1 hr.

Directions   **Put In**—N.C. 16 about 8.5 mi. north of U.S. 421, to Rt. 1546 and then east about .5 mi. to a gravel pit. This is private property, so observe it as such.

Take Out—Grade road immediately east of U.S. 421-A bridge, and north to North Wilkesboro city limits, which is beyond city sewage treatment plant.

Stony Fork Creek

Stony Fork Creek

The Stony Fork runs off of the slopes of Tompkins Knob, off the Blue Ridge Parkway, and winds its way between Dividing Ridge and Elk Ridge, before confluencing with the Yadkin River above Kerr Scott Reservoir.

It is a small, fast moving stream, dropping over many small ledges.

It might be worth noting that it was in this area, between the Stony Fork and Elk Creek, that Tom Dula of "Hang Down Your Head" fame supposedly did his dastardly deed.

Topo Map   Grandin, Boomer

County   Wilkes

(1)   Wilkes Co. Rt. 1155 (Mt. Zion Rd.) to Rt. 1137, on Kerr Scott Lake

Drop	Difficulty	Distance	Time	Scenery	Water Quality
89′	1-2/4	6 mi.	3 hrs.	A	Good

Gage   On the northeast side of Rt. 1135 bridge (Mt. Pleasant Rd.) facing west. Minimum for solo is 6″ below the bottom of "0." Generally is runnable during wet seasons.

Difficulties   Primarily ledges of 1 ft. to 18 in. high, until just above the Yadkin, where it drops considerably faster. This can be recognized by a large tree, which blocks most of the river. Directly behind it on the right, most of the stream pours down a 4 ft. drop into a great deal of turbulence and continues on down through a boulder garden. The total drop is some 9-10 ft. within about 50 ft.

Directions   **Put In**—From U.S. 421 go approximately 9 mi. west of Wilkesboro, to Rt. 1154, then south to Rt. 1155 and left approximately 2 mi. to the put in, just above a bridge crossing a small stream coming into the Stony Fork.

From Ferguson on N.C. 268 go northwest on Rt. 1135 (which becomes 1158 after crossing the Stony Fork) to Rt. 1155 and left approximately 2mi.

Take Out—3.9 mi. east of Ferguson on N.C. 268 to Wilkes Rt. 1137, and north 1.5 mi. to the lake.

Approximately .75 mi., mostly backwaters, can be eliminated by taking out up a rather steep bank along N.C. 268, about 2.5 mi. east of Ferguson.

Yadkin River

Yadkin River

The Yadkin heads up in the mountain resort town of Blowing Rock and flows through a remote mountainous area of Caldwell County before coming alongside U.S. 321 about 3 mi. north of Patterson. It moves generally northeasterly through Happy Valley into Kerr Scott Lake, and then meanders through 5 counties before entering the impoundment at High Rock Lake in Davidson County. Two additional impoundments, Badin and Tillery, follow immediately after which the Yadkin becomes the PeeDee and flows into South Carolina.

The river is primarily pastoral down from Patterson, moving over occasional low ledges and through shallow rock gardens. Below Kerr Scott dam it continues on much the same, although considerably wider and with fewer rapids, until it makes the big bend to the south below Siloam. Here, it drops fairly fast for a couple of miles over a series of shoals, which can become formidable in medium high waters.

The one other point of difficulty on the river is Idols Dam, which is downstream from I-40 bridge and just below Tanglewood Park. Water flows over the dam and it should be approached with great caution.

Naturally, a water way crossing as much of a state as the Yadkin does carries with it much history—in fact, too much to delve into here in any detail. However, in section (3) it is of interest to note that the Daniel Boone family had two home sites in the vicinity in the 1760s. The first was near Beaver Creek, about .75 mi. south of the river, where the hearth still stands; the second was on the north side of the river just below the mouth of Beaver Creek. It was from here that Boone left on his trek to Kentucky in April 1775.

Topo Maps   Buffalo Cove, Lenoir, Grandin, Boomer

Counties   Caldwell, Wilkes

(1)   N.C. 268 bridge at Patterson to N.C. 268 bridge

Drop	Difficulty	Distance	Time	Scenery	Water Quality
53'	1-2	4.2 mi.	2 hrs.	B	Fair

Gage   U.S.G.S. gage is located 50 yds. above N.C. 268 bridge in Patterson, on the east bank. Minimum reading for solo is 1.28.

Difficulties   None, but the river narrows considerably just below the put in, so the possibility of blocked passages always exists.

(2) N.C. 268 bridge northeast of Patterson School to Rt. 1509 bridge

Drop	Difficulty	Distance	Time	Scenery	Water Quality
59′	1-2	6.2 mi.	2.5 hrs.	B	Fair

Gage   Can be run all year. Would be tight through a couple of shoals in very dry periods.

Difficulties   None.

(3) Caldwell Co. Rt. 1509 bridge (Grandin Rd.) to the end of Wilkes Co. Rt. 1137 on Kerr Scott Lake

Drop	Difficulty	Distance	Time	Scenery	Water Quality
29′	1-2	9.5 mi.	4 hrs.	B	Fair

Gage   Can be run all year.

Difficulties   None.

Directions   **Put In**—N.C. 268 N.E. off U.S. 321 north of Lenoir.
Take Out—3.9 mi. east of the community of Ferguson, on N.C. 268 to Wilkes Co. Rt. 1137 and north 1.5 mi. to the lake.

Yadkin River

Section 5

Chattooga River

Chattooga River

The Chattooga rises as a sparkling mountain stream near Cashiers, N.C., in the vicinity of Whitesides Mountain. It flows 10 mi. before leaving North Carolina, and continuing on for some 40 mi. as the boundary line between South Carolina and Georgia, before entering the impoundment at Lake Tugaloo. In this 50 mi. the river drops 2,469 ft., for an average drop of 49.3 ft./mi.

The river cuts down the magnificent Chattooga Gorge, providing many rugged white water cascades through an area which is almost totally wild and natural. Upon reaching Nicholson Fields, above Rt. 28, it becomes a more pastoral area and continues as such to Turn Hole. Beyond there, it slowly begins to revert back to its wild and rugged characteristics and is accessible at only five points within the next 24 mi.

It is one of the longest and largest free flowing rivers in the southeast and is the only mountain river in a four state area without substantial development along its banks. Its outstanding scenery and unspoiled wilderness will now be protected with its inclusion as the second National Wild and Scenic River, under Public Law 90-542. With this protection the river hopefully will be preserved in a natural state for generations to come, so that they may see what their forefathers saw—a wild and free flowing river. In order to continue this preservation, certain conditions must be followed:

1. Each float party leader must register.
2. All floaters, including innertubers, must wear a life jacket rated "Coast Guard Approved."
3. All persons in decked craft, and ALL floaters below Woodalls Shoals, must wear a helmet.
4. Minimum party size:
   Above Earls Ford—2 persons, 1 craft
   Below Earls Ford—2 persons, 2 craft
5. Innertubes are prohibited below Earls Ford
6. Rafts must have a minimum of 2 air chambers
7. All floating is prohibited north of S.C. Hwy. 28.
8. Air mattresses, motorized craft, or other craft deemed unsuitable by the U.S. Forest Service, are prohibited.

The following conditions have been established for camping:
1. 50 ft. from river, stream, or hiking trail
2. .25 mi. from a maintained road
3. 200 yds. from any other occupied site
4. 15 persons maximum occupancy.

The stream that heretofore had been known to a few trout fishermen, backpackers, and canoeists has been made famous by the film "Deliverance." It brings many canoeists and rafters to the river, who know little of what to expect and who quite often are ill equipped to handle what they find. It is for this reason that the author has gone into greater detail in describing certain rapids in the river than has been done on other rivers. Hopefully such knowledge will persuade the unprepared adventure seeker to reconsider and arm himself with the skill that the Chattooga demands of those who seek her unspoiled beauty.

Topo Maps   Satolah, Rainy Mtn., Tugaloo Lake (Ga.); Whetstone (Ga.-S.C.)

Counties   Oconee (S.C.); Rabun (Ga.)

Section (1)

The stretch from Burrels Ford to Rt. 28 bridge, usually referred to as Section (1), has not been included because of the extreme gradient of the upper part of the section. Also, floating above Rt. 28 is prohibited at this time by the Forest Service.

(2)   Rt. 28 bridge (Russell Bridge) to Earls Ford

Drop	Difficulty	Distance	Time	Scenery	Water Quality
80′	1-2/3	7 mi.	3.5 hrs.	A	Good

Gage   Metal gage on Georgia side of Rt. 28 bridge. A minimum reading of .72 and a maximum of 2.23 indicate the optimum levels.

Difficulties   The water is generally shallow and slow to the mouth of the West Fork where the current picks up.

Long Bottom Bridge, about 2.5 mi. downstream, must be carried, so the novice paddler should approach with care.

Turn Hole is the first rapid of any consequence. Here the water pushes the canoe into the left bank and a strong pull to the right is necessary in order to stay out of the branches. Following Turn Hole is a series of rapids which require one to maneuver back and forth across the streambed.

Big Shoals, the Class 3, can be recognized by the big rock ledges which appear to block most of the center and left side. The run is to the far right through an open chute which twists slightly to the left at the bottom. The drop is about 5 ft. Scout from the ledge in the center and carry over there is necessary.

Small riffles and shoals continue on down to just above Earls Ford where passage becomes a little more complex. Beginners and novices should not attempt to continue beyond here.

Directions **Put In**—S.C.-Ga. 28 bridge.
Take Out—From Mountain Rest, S.C. on S.C. 28 go southwest on Rt. 258 which becomes Rt. 196 to the first 4-way stop intersection and bear right to the end of pavement and beyond on graded road to the river and Earls Ford. There is a 1,400 ft. carry from the river to the parking area.

(3) Earls Ford to U.S. 76 bridge

Drop	Difficulty	Distance	Time	Scenery	Water Quality
370'	3-4-5	12.5 mi.	6 hrs.	AA	Good

Gage U.S.G.S. gage 75 yds. downstream from 76 bridge on the S.C. side. A reading of 1.3 to 2.0 is considered a minimum and maximum for open boats.

Difficulties and Points of Interest The second rapid below Earls Ford should be entered on the left side of the river, then turn hard left dropping over a 3 ft. ledge which in lower water levels puts the bow on a rock just under the surface at the bottom. This gives the paddler a quick idea of whether he should be here or not. If trouble occurs here it is not too late to head back, for several rapids follow that are much more difficult.

About 400 yds. beyond, the river passes through Rock Gardens, where great slabs of angular rock stick up out of the river. Several scenes in "Deliverance" were filmed here.

The next rapid of any consequence is Dick's Creek ledge, which is recognized by Five Finger Falls cascading down on the Georgia side. Scout on the right center, which is also the best place to portage. For those wishing to run this, an "S" turn is required. The first drop should be entered with the bow angled to the right as the canoe slides down the ledge and drops into the small pool above the next ledge. Do not attempt to enter from the left side at the top.

The next two rapids should be run to the right of the respective islands. Below these rapids is Sandy Ford, which is the last place to take out for those who find the river more than they can handle. There is a very rough road negotiable only by four wheel drive vehicles, on the Georgia side.

Mild rapids follow, and then a calm pool before the river bears left. Around the bend is the Narrows, where three concentric ledges funnel the river into a constricted canyon. Enter toward the left. Two more drops follow as the river narrows down even more. Beware of the turbulent cross currents below these drops. More canoes swamp here than at any other point on the river. It is very difficult to get through the entrance ledges without swamping if paddling tandem. A beautiful cliff overhangs the river below the last drop. This makes an excellent lunch stop.

Second Ledge is around the next bend. Scout or portage it on the right. This can be run on the left side by sliding down across the face of the falls, not too easy by any means. At higher levels, a run down right center, if possible, with a hard right turn into the pool, eddy turn, then drop through a small slot in the bottom ledge.

Eye of the Needle, about 1.5 mi. beyond Second Ledge, is entered on the extreme left. A rock ledge extends about halfway across the river from the right, forcing most of the water through a twisting chute dropping to the right. Don't lean to the right and you'll arrive upright. Note to decked boats: there is a good spot for "pop ups" at the bottom.

There are some four miles of easy rapids before arriving at Fall Creek Falls, entering on the left.

Just below the falls is the Roller Coaster, a delightful ride through a series of big waves, and also a very good place for the unwary to fill the craft.

The next rapid is a large ledge called Keyhole. Scout on the left. Enter on the right center and cut to the right. A very large boulder sits on the left center in the bottom. If entering to the left, a mishap can push a boat square into the rock.

There are several interesting ledges and shoals in the next 3 mi., before arriving at a bend to the left. A huge rock formation extending from the right bank is just beyond. This marks the entrance rapid to Bull Sluice, a series of two falls totaling 10 ft. in height. The rock formation and large boulders block the "Sluice" from view, so immediately upon spotting the bend and the rocks pull out on the right. Portage on the right also.

The entrance rapid to Bull Sluice is a class 3, which can splash a great deal of water into the canoe before ever arriving at the first falls. The hydraulic below the first falls can easily hold a body or a boat in, so give it all due respect. The second has a rock just under the surface which is generally well hidden. What appears as a fast open chute isn't. The author broke a rib bouncing off this rock, and on another occasion saw a swamped 17 ft. Grumman do an end over end when the bow met with said rock. So if attempting to run Bull Sluice, don't assume that it's been made if one makes it beyond the hydraulic. Keep in mind that several drownings have occurred here.

U.S. 76 bridge is about 300 yds. downstream around the bend. For those who wish to see the "Sluice" before or without running the river, a trail leads up along the S.C. side.

Directions   **Put In**—From U.S. 76 bridge, go east approximately 2 mi. to the first paved road on the left (S.C. 196). Proceed north approximately 6 mi. to the first 4-way stop intersection. Bear left there on S.C. 193, which becomes a graded road, until reaching the parking area, some 1,400 ft. above Earls Ford and the river. You guessed it, neighbor, you get to warm up before you reach the water.

From S.C. 28 go west on S.C. 193 (2 mi. south of the intersection of 28 and S.C. 107), and proceed to the river on 193.

Take Out—From the put in, backtrack on the above directions. (Take the first two paved roads to the right, coming from Earls Ford Parking Area). Hopefully, you've got a little energy left, for now you get to "cool down" with your second 1,400 ft. hike of the day, to the parking area at 76 bridge.

Chattooga, Section (4)

(94)   U.S. 76 bridge to Tugaloo Lake

Drop	Difficulty	Distance	Time	Scenery	Water Quality
275'	3-4-5	7.5 mi.	5 hrs.	AA	Fair

Gage   U.S.G.S. gage. A reading from 1.1. to 1.9 is considered a minimum and a maximum for open boats.

Difficulties and Points of Interest   This section offers the paddler some of the most beautiful and challenging white water in the east. There are many rapids throughout the stretch which an intermediate would find difficult, but only the major falls and rapids will be discussed. In other words, only those rapids that will prove difficult to even the advanced canoeist will be mentioned.

The first, Surfing Rapid, is entered from the right after coming around the first bend of the river below the put in.

Some distance downstream, a large sandbar appears on the Georgia side. About 200 yds. below is Rock Jumble, a single drop which is clutted with rock. Scout to determine the best place to run.

About .5 mi. downstream, where the river bends left, a large rock ledge extends out from the S.C. side, forcing the water to the right. Pull out on the ledge before the current does the same to the canoe, and scout. At the end of this ledge is the entrance falls to Woodall Shoals. It forms a strong, dangerous hydraulic at the bottom, which has kept boats, rafts, people, or anything else that floats, for extended periods of time. Due to the power of the hydraulic, this is probably the most dangerous spot on the river. It definitely is not the place to play. At lower water levels a slanting ledge on the far right might be run without the danger the hydraulic presents.

The rest of the Shoals is a twisting turning ride for another 60 yds. before ending in a quiet pool. A very rough forest road enters into Woodall on the S.C. side.

Below the Shoals the river enters a gorge containing two fairly long rapids with standing waves. Let this be the warning of Seven-Foot Falls coming up. Scout it on the right, where instead of the abrupt drop of the left, a slanting drop can be run.

Following several rapids, the river widens and Stekoa Creek drops in from the right, indicating the beginning of Stekoa Creek Rapids, a quarter mile of constant white water. The creek is the source of the pollution that has prevented the rest of the section from qualifying in the Wild, Scenic, or Recreation River class, but hopefully this will soon be remedied by a new sewage treatment plant. It has been listed in a Conditional Scenic River class.

Long Creek Falls, a beautiful waterfall which was shown in "Deliverance," enters on the left into the pool at the end of Stekoa Creek Rapids.

Following several ledges the river runs into a house-size boulder. It has become known as "Deliverance Rock" due to several scenes in the movie having been shot here.

A beautiful cliff, Raven Rock, rises on the left high above the river, as one paddles beyond "Deliverance Rock." Just above the cliff is Raven Rock Rapid, which should be scouted on the left and run on the far left across the face of the slanting rock.

For a little over a mile, the river courses over small rapids which appropriately enough have been called "Calm Before the Storm." Below here the river pulls out all stops as it enters The Five Falls, one of the most exciting stretches of water to be found anywhere.

1. First Fall is entered down a long stubblefield running diagonally left to far right into a small pool. At this point it is best to scout, perhaps the rest of the falls, before continuing. First Fall should be run on the right and angling to the

left. If trouble develops upon attempting First Fall, get to shore immediately, because 100 ft. downstream is

2. Corkscrew, which is the toughest rapid for an open boat on the river, and is a mass of surging cross currents. It cannot be run without swamping. Carry on the right.

3. Crack in the Rock, which in reality is 3 cracks, follows. The five foot crack on the right is the safest of the three, although it can be dangerous as it sometimes becomes partially clogged by logs and debris. Scout on the right. There is a good pool for rescue below the crack. Avoid "left crack" at all costs. Two boaters have drowned there in recent years.

4. Jawbone comes up next. Scout on the left. It should be entered from right center. Drop left into the eddy on the far left, make an eddy turn and then cut back into the main chute to be flushed out at the bottom. At the bottom the main current runs into and by a large boulder on the left, but it is best to cut out of the current to the right above the boulder and then paddle back into the eddy on the left below it, to look over

5. Sock 'Em Dog, a 7 ft. vertical drop on the far right. Jawbone in itself isn't terribly difficult, but with Sock 'Em Dog awaiting to chew up a swamped craft, one must consider carefully before attempting the run. The eddy on the left is the best spot to get out from to scout or to carry. The run is to the far right over a slight rise at the very top of the falls. For those who can't resist the temptation, there is a long pool to reassemble whatever needs be.

The last rapid of any consequence above the lake, Shoulder Bone, is at the end of the pool. Run it at left center. After that one can relax somewhat before the fun beings—a 2 mi. paddle down Lake Tugaloo.

Directions   **Put In**—At the U.S. 76 bridge.

Take Out—Go east on U.S. 76 to the community of Longcreek and take a right on S.C. 96. Proceed on 96, which turns to gravel and then back to pavement, until Damascus Church is passed on the left. Take the next right (Forest Rd. 754) and on to Tugaloo Lake, over one hellacious bumpy single lane road. In the event the above road is impassable due to inclement weather, take out can be made by paddling 2 mi. farther down the lake to the dam on the Georgia side. Off U.S. 23, about .5 mi. south of Tallulah Falls, go east on the road to the hydroelectric plant.

Chauga River, S.C.

Chauga River, S.C.

The Chauga heads up on the eastern slopes of Chattooga Ridge in Sumter National Forest, wherein flow the first two sections. It moves south, then sharply east and south again, until it reaches the backwaters of Lake Hartwell. On its way it cuts through several small gorges that rival the Chattooga River for spectacular beauty.

Section (2), known as the "Chauga Gorge," begins with gentle rapids in the first mile, before dropping quickly through a series of waterfalls and continuous fast water. Access is difficult so the paddler should be skilled enough to handle his boat under very rough water conditions as well as care for any emergencies that might arise.

Topo Maps   Whetstone, Holly Springs

County   Oconee

(1)   Oconee Co. Rt. 193 bridge (Blackwell Bridge) to Rt. 290 bridge

Drop	Difficulty	Distance	Time	Scenery	Water Quality
206' 2 mi. @ 63'/mi.	2-3	5.4 mi.	3.5 hrs.	A	Good

Gage   Oconee Co. Rt. 290 bridge. Minimum run for solo is 2" above "0." The gage on U.S. 76 bridge on the Chattooga will require a reading of 2.3.

Difficulties   Within the first .5 mi. there is a 45 ft. waterfall, which can be carried on the right. It is followed by a 10 ft. sliding drop that can be run at slightly higher water levels. One should watch for downed trees throughout the section.

(2)   Oconee Co. Rt. 290 bridge (Cassidy Bridge) to Cobbs Bridge Road bridge. (Take the first right .75 mi. north of Holly Springs community)

Drop	Difficulty	Distance	Time	Scenery	Water Quality
417' 1 mi. @ 140'/mi.	3-4-5	9.8 mi.	7 hrs.	AA	Good

Gage   Oconee Co. Rt. 290 bridge. Minimum for solo run is "0.". Maximum for a safe run is 6".

Difficulties Watch for downed trees within the first mile. As one enters the gorge, watch for a waterfall which should be carried on the left. Approximately 1 mi. further on is another falls, that can possibly be run at a favorable level. The river continues to drop quickly as it turns toward the east. A slanting waterfall, which is best carried, is followed by continuous heavy water for close to 2 mi. Several Class 3 rapids are interspersed along the way, as the gradient eases up for a couple of miles. Then, some 2 mi. above the take out, a sheer falls is reached, that requires a carry on the right.

(3) Cobb Bridge Rd. bridge to Co. Rt. 34 bridge (Horseshoe Bend Bridge)

Drop	Difficulty	Distance	Time	Scenery	Water Quality
135'	2-3/4	7.5 mi.	4.5 hrs.	A-B	Good

Gage   U.S. 76 bridge on the Chattooga. Minimum for a solo run is 1.8. Maximum for a safe run is 2.5.

Difficulties Below the U.S. 76 bridge and just above the water pumping facility is Pumphouse, a Class 3 which can be scouted from the rocks in left center. Just downstream is the Class 4, Canopener—a steep 5 ft. slide with a sharp rock alongside the chute that can "open" one's boat up if not careful. Scout it before running.

Directions   **Put In**—N.E. on Oconee Co. Rt. 196 off U.S. 76, for 6.1 mi. to Whetstone and the intersection with Rt. 193. Take a right to the bridge.
Take Out—S.W. on Oconee Co. Rt. 34 off U.S. 76, west of Westminster.

Doe River

The Doe flows off Roan Mountain, through the town of the same name, and cuts through the spectacular Doe River Gorge on its way to join the Watauga in Elizabethton, Tennessee. The Gorge, between Fork Mountain on the south and Cedar Mountain on the north, is 800-1,000 ft. deep. There are several outstanding rock formations, the most prominent being Flagpole Point, jutting out sharply on the right, and Pardee Point, rising high on the left.

A small gage railroad, where the original "Tweetsie" of the East Tennessee and Western North Carolina ran, makes it fairly easy to scout the gorge on foot. In fact, this is recommended in order for one to fully appreciate the rugged beauty. A hike down the gorge is highly recommended for those who haven't the skill to paddle it.

Topo Maps   White Rocks Mtn., Iron Mtn. Gap, Elizabethton (Tenn.)

County   Carter (Tenn.)

(1)   U.S. 19E at the confluence with Buck Creek to U.S. 19E bridge

Drop	Difficulty	Distance	Time	Scenery	Water Quality
55'	1-2	2.6 mi.	1 hr.	B-C	Good

Gage   U.S.G.S. gage on section (2). Take the road east of Honeycutt Grocery. Minimum reading of 3.80 for solo run. Can be run all year except after dry spells.

Difficulties   None.

(2)   U.S. 19E bridge at Crabtree, to the bridge at Blevins

Drop	Difficulty	Distance	Time	Scenery	Water Quality
182'	2-3/4	4.6 mi.	3 hrs.	A-B	Good
1 mi. @ 65'/mi.					

Gage   Minimum reading of 4.14 for solo.

Doe River

Difficulties   There are two Class 4 rapids in the second mile. Both should be approached cautiously and scouted to determine if a passage is open. Each is strewn with boulders and has a difficult entrance.

(3)   Bridge at Blevins (off 19E at Whitehead Hill) to U.S. 19E bridge at Hampton

Drop	Difficulty	Distance	Time	Scenery	Water Quality
498'	3-4-5/6	6 mi.	6 hrs.	AA-A	Good
1 mi. @ 145'/mi.					
2 mi. @ 115'/mi.					

Gage   4.30 for solo. Maximum reading of 4.70. Due to the gradient and tight passages the river courses through, not much leeway between the minimum and maximum is left.

Difficulties   The road at the put in continues along the river for 2.5 mi. to the head of the railroad tracks. The upper section can be scouted from the road. There is one Class 4 above the first railroad bridge, where the water piles up on a rock, requiring a hard left turn into a drop of 3-4 ft.

Below the first railroad bridge there are numerous rapids, many of which require scouting. Be on the lookout for a point where the river bends to the right, where the entrace is pretty well clogged up. Below here a 75 yd. carry on the left must be made. This area is impassable in an open boat, but the thrill seeker may wish to put back in just above the bottom to try the 7 ft. falls on the right.

Following the falls, the next hairy rapid can be recognized by the rock wall constructed to support the railroad tracks. Here a series of diagonal ledges make for an extremely difficult course.

As the river approaches the next rock wall, the course splits into two channels with a Class 6 on the left, and on the right a jumble of boulders. Line down on the right. One unwary paddler swamped twice here, just portaging.

From here to the take out, there are many exciting rapids remaining, several of which should be scouted. This section is not recommended for the paddler who is not in excellent condition. The stress and strain are sure to take their toll on one who isn't.

212

(4) U.S. 19E bridge south of Hampton to U.S. 19E bridge in Elizabethton

Drop	Difficulty	Distance	Time	Scenery	Water Quality
252'	2-3	9.5 mi.	4.5 hrs.	A-B-C	Fair
2 mi. @ 50'/mi.					

Gage   Minimum reading of 4.20 for solo.

Difficulties   A Class 3 directly beneath the first 19E bridge north of Hampton may require scouting. Beyond the second bridge a series of ledges form a staircase which will require a good deal of maneuvering to locate the best passage. Other than these there are a few stubblefields which one should watch for.

Directions   **Put In**—U.S. 19E below confluence with Buck Creek and east of Tennessee Rt. 143 in the town of Roan Mountain.
Take Out—Power Sub Station 100 yds. above U.S. 19E bridge over the Watauga River, on the south bank in Elizabethton.

Elk River

Elk River

The Elk flows out of Avery County, North Carolina, forming the Elk River Gorge as it enters the state of Tennessee. It contains a large number of falls, notably Big Falls, located at the end of Avery Co Rt. 1305; and Twisting Falls, about 1 mi. above the suggested put in. The river drops 160 ft. in little more than .5 mi. in the Twisting Falls area. This is a very scenic run through rugged terrain. There are many ledges to give the canoeist an exciting trip.

Topo Map   Elk Mills (Tenn.)

County   Carter (Tenn.)

(1)   Bridge below Stone Mountain Church to U.S. 321 bridge

Drop	Difficulty	Distance	Time	Scenery	Water Quality
212'	2-3	5.5 mi.	3 hrs.	A	Good
1 mi. @ 55'/mi.					

Gage   Northeast side of U.S. 321 bridge. Minimum for solo run is 6" below "0.". Runnable most of the year, except during long dry spells. Best in spring and early summer.

Difficulties   There are several ledges that may require scouting through the area of the greatest drop. This stretch is located downstream from the second bridge and can be recognized by the bluffs which rise some 300 ft. above the river.

Directions   **Put In**—From U.S. 321, south on the first paved road east of 321 bridge over the Elk. Go through the community of Elk Mills to the second bridge.
Take Out—Below U.S. 321 bridge at Elk Mills.

Haw River

Haw River

The Haw River begins in the northwest corner of Guilford County, flows east around Greensboro and Burlington, turning generally southeast. It meets the New Hope River in Chatham County, where the Cape Fear River is born. The Haw varies greatly in width, from 50 ft. in some sections to as much as 1,000 ft. at the dam at Bynum.

The river flows through farm lands, forested hills and some residential areas. As with most rivers in the lower Piedmont, there are long stretches of flat water to be paddled, as well as the many rapids. There are many places where the river branches into two or more channels, each island looking very much like the last one, long, narrow, and heavily covered with trees, shrubs, brambles, and poison ivy.

Author's note: Some of this description is no longer accurate since much of the bank below 64 bridge has been stripped by that most efficient raper of mother nature, the U.S. Corps of Engineers. The B. Everett Jordan Dam will involve some 44,000 acres including some of the finest wildlife habitat and farm land in the Piedmont of North Carolina. The only hope that section (2) will not be innundated is that somewhere along the way the impossible may happen and the Corps might be forced to operate this area as a dry lake. Overwhelming evidence has been presented that the lake will be something short of a cesspool for many years and perhaps forever, but the Corps has gone on selling it as a tremendous water recreation resource. (From the notes of Bob Loddengaard.)

Topo Maps   Bynum, New Hope Dam

County   Chatham

(1)   Chatham Co. Rt. 1545 bridge ("Chicken Bridge") to the dam, just upstream of U.S. 15-501 bridge

Drop	Difficulty	Distance	Time	Scenery	Water Quality
50'	1-2	6.5 mi.	3 hrs.	A-B	Fair

Gage   There is no convenient gage for this section of the river. A good guide, however, is to see how many of the bridge's footings are visible. If three can be seen, the river is low, and the trip will be long. When none may be seen, the river should not be run by novices. When the river rises to within 2-3 ft. of the concrete cross braces, it should not be run by anyone. This section can be run year around except following an unusually long dry season.

Difficulties   There are only two places of any consequence. The first is about 1.7 mi. downstream, where the river makes an abrupt left turn and goes around an island. The rapid on the right is normally entered as close to the island as the overhanging branches will allow. The second rapid is about 4 mi. downstream, after about a mile of pleasant and nearly continuous rapids. The river is quite wide, with an island placed to the left. At low water it is run to the left and once past the island, the rapids should be traversed to the right, to avoid a large boulder about 100 yds. downstream. Only one more rapid remains; downstream of the gas line, where the lake starts. Stay on the left side of the river to the take out just upstream of the dam.

(2)   U.S. 15-501 bridge, on the south side of the river, and upstream of the bridge to Rt. 1943 bridge

Drop	Difficulty	Distance	Time	Scenery	Water Quality
117'	1-2-3	6 mi.	2.5 hrs.	A-B	Fair

Gage   The gage is located on an upstream piling on the north side of U.S. 64 bridge. Minimum for solo is 6" below "0.". Maximum is 1.5 above "0."

Difficulties   There are many parallel paths which can be taken, but generally the widest part of the river is best for the newcomer. Once past the bridge at Bynum (visible from U.S. 15-501 bridge), one should traverse the river far to the left. A mile from the put in, the river will be narrow and present three choices of direction. The left channel has a Class 2+ drop consisting of a ledge and rapids immediately below. It is best run through a chute just to the left of the small island, although at high water it can be approached in the center, with a quick "S" turn required after the first drop.

After some miles, the river becomes flat and very wide. When the water level is higher than "0," the canoeist can paddle to the right, passing through many rocks and tiny islands and taking a series of delightful drops at the extreme right of the river. At the end of these drops there is a Class 2+, an "S" turn, requiring a hard left turn. (At the aforementioned spot one can also elect to remain to the left, going through a long run over a rock field, and approach the center of the U.S. Rt. 64 bridge). Below 64 bridge, one can remain at the right or go through a narrow slot between two islands about 50 yds. downstream of the bridge, to get out into the main channel. (The paddler continuing from the left channel may elect to take the right hand route, by moving close to the right just before the bridge, and turning back upsteam through the narrow slot.)

The advantage of the right channel is that the Lunch Stop Rapid, Class 3, can be run. It is most difficult at low water and is run close to the right, moving to the left just at the bottom to avoid a rock.

Fifty yards below the Lunch Stop Rapid, a left is taken to move out into the main current. The water is heavy with large standing waves. After a run of 200-300 yds., there is a sharp turn to the left, followed immediately by a hard right, to get into calm water just upstream of Gabriel's Bend.

Gabriel's Bend, a Class 3+, is identified by a high rock wall on the right, and may be scouted on the right. Open boats may run it anywhere with the gage of "0" or less. At higher levels the standing waves become large and holes develop, which can easily swamp a canoe. The conservative route is close to the left all the way, and very close to the large rock halfway down.

Immediately below Gabriel's Bend, the paddler traverses all the way to the left of the river through some islands where the Haw's Revenge, a Class 3, awaits. It cannot be seen from above and because of the banks and fast current, is very hard to scout. It should be entered to the left under overhanging branches, working to keep from being swept to the right. Remain to the left past a large jagged rock, and at the bottom go through some small rocks. The temptation is to take a right before the innocent looking rocks. Firmly resist, as many boats have been badly mangled there.

The next major drop is approached from the left side of the river and has a number of possible entries. At a gage reading of 1 ft., a straight chute appears at the left of a small island. Below that level, one enters at the left but moves quickly to the right of the island, traversing all the way across, exiting at the far right.

After a small but pesky ledge, and a wide open area with a continuous but gradual drop, the Pipeline, a Class 3, is found by remaining generally to the right of the open river, where a straight and fairly narrow section separates off on the right. At the end, there is a turn to the right, entering the Pipeline. Standing waves are large and holes develop at high gage readings. Near the end, the rapid does a quick "S" to the right, going around a large boulder located on the left. Unfortunately for the paddler, when the river is running high the cofferdam downstream of the take out will create a lake, which often backs up to cover the Pipeline.

The steel bridge can be seen once one is out of the Pipeline, with the take out on the left directly at the bridge.

Directions   **Put In**—Go west off U.S. 15-501 (1.4 mi. north of the Haw River
bridge) on Chatham Co. Rt. 1525 for 4.3 mi. Turn sharp left at
the intersection, remaining on Rt. 1525 for 2.8 mi. Turn left again on Rt. 1545
for 1 mi. to the "Chicken Bridge." Put in on the south side, downstream of the
bridge.

Take Out—Go east off U.S. 15-501 (2.9 mi. north of U.S. 15-
501 Haw River bridge) on Rt. 1700 for 4.4 mi. Cross U.S. 64
and continue on Rt. 1700 for another 1.7 mi. Turn right on a dirt road, Rt.
1941 for 1 mi. Then shift to a paved road, keeping right on Rt. 1943 for .3 mi.
to the steel bridge.

Author's Note: There have been quite a few incidents of paddlers running
below 64 bridge at rather high water levels with disastrous results. The local
rescue squads and law enforcement agencies have spent many hours aiding
these victims of their own poor judgement. Local citizens have actually asked
that the river be closed to canoeists due to the strain on the county finances.
Don't fan the fires further by putting in at a questionable level. If in doubt,
check the gage.

■

*Like winds and sunsets, wild things were taken for granted until progress
began to do away with them.*   *Aldo Leopold*

North Tyger and Tyger River

The north Tyger heads up in northern Spartanburg County and flows practically the length of the county, to where we pick it up just upstream of the confluence with the South Tyger. It drops through the Fall Line, presenting several miles of interesting white water. This area is composed of long pools, with occasional sharp drops and long shoals.

Topo Maps   Spartanburg, Enoree

Counties   Spartanburg

(1)   Spartanburg Co. Rt. 231 bridge over the North Tyger to Spartanburg Co. Rt. 113 bridge over the Tyger

Drop	Difficulty	Distance	Time	Scenery	Water Quality
76'	2-3	7.6 mi.	3.5 hr.	A	Good-Fair

Gage   Spartanburg Co. Rt. 231 bridge at the northwest corner. Minimum for solo is 8" below "0."

Difficulties   This stretch is primarily a series of pools interspersed with ledges and long shoals, several of which can be quite formidable at higher water levels (above 1 on the gage). The second rapid drops 7 ft. in some 25 yds. and has a rather sneaky hydraulic in the center that one must punch through.

Nesbitt Shoals runs for about 200 yds. above Rt. 50 bridge. Below the bridge one encounters another 150 yds. of shoals which should be run right of center, due to a number of large rods in the middle and far left immediately below the first ledge. The last shoals run .25 mi. down to the take out. It has many possible passages.

(2)   Spartanburg Co. Rt. 113 bridge to S.C. 56 bridge

Drop	Difficulty	Distance	Time	Scenery	Water Quality
45'	C-1-2-3/4	6.2 mi.	3 hrs.	A	Good-Fair

Gage   Spartanburg Co. Rt. 113 bridge on the southwest corner. Minimum for solo run is 8" below "0."

Difficulties A series of shoals run for almost a half mile, providing many choices of channels. This stretch ends with a natural 6 ft. vertical dam. Approach with great caution, for at higher levels, one will have a very difficuilt time scouting this ledge. Beyond this point, one will encounter primarily fast flatwater.

Directions **Put In**—S.C. 86 south of U.S. 221 to Spartanburg Co. Rt. 231, then east across I-26 to the bridge.
Take Out—South off S.C. 50 on Spartanburg Co. Rt. 142, then northeast on Spartanburg Co. Rt. 113 to the river.

North Tyger and Tyger River
South Tyger River, South Carolina

South Tyger River, South Carolina

The South Tyger heads up in the foothills and cuts across the Piedmont Plateau before making its final plunge where we pick it up. This section has long pools with occasional sharp drops, that make the flatter stretches worth paddling.

Topo Maps   Spartanburg, Enoree

County   Spartanburg

(1)   Spartanburg Co. Rt. 86 bridge over Fergusons Creek to S.C. 50 bridge over the Tyger

Drop	Difficulty	Distance	Time	Scenery	Water Quality
36'	2-3	5.2 mi.	1.75 hr.	A	Fair

Gage   Spartanburg Co. Rt. 231 bridge on the North Tyger at the northwest corner. Minimum for solo run is 8" below "0."

Difficulties   Susan Thomas Shoals drops 5.5 ft. in about 30 yds. It can be scouted at right center. The next shoals, Chesnee, now known as "Stingemdog" due to an experience Jack and David Powell had with their canine companion, presents a very technical run. The rapid drops 7 ft. within 50 yds. It can be scouted far left. Nesbitt Shoals runs for some 200 yds. just below the confluence with the North Tyger and continues on to the take out.

Directions   **Put In**—Go north on Spartanburg Co. Rt. 86 off S.C. to Fergusons Creek bridge, and put in alongside 86.
   Take Out—S.C. 50 bridge east of I-26. For an extended trip of 3.3 mi. down the Tyger to Spartanburg Co. Rt. 113, see Section (1) of the North Tyger and Tyger.

Section 6

Introduction

This section includes primarily flatter water suitable for canoe camping trips. Over the years the author has been asked about suitable stretches of water that beginning and novice paddlers can handle in canoes loaded with camping gear. The Broad and two of its tributaries—the Enoree and the Tyger—contains approximately 220 mi. from which beginner and novice paddlers can select trips. The description of the tributaries continues into the Broad in order to give Boy Scout troups two separate streams for possible 50-miler trips.

The Enoree is the easiest of the three rivers. The Tyger requires slightly more river skill, while the Broad is more difficult, from the standpoint of both skill and strength needed to negotiate the rapids as well as the dams.

All three flow through remote areas for most of the distance, with little signs of civilization evidenced except at bridges and dams. Wildlife is exceptional along the Enoree and the Tyger in particular. The author has observed as large a variety of wildlife along these stretches as any he has paddled, and in great abundance.

For those considering a trip on the tributaries or one including the lower Broad, we recommend obtaining a map of the Enoree and Tyger Districts of the Sumter National Forest, which is available from the District Ranger in either Newberry or Union, South Carolina.

Please note that paddle times listed are conservative, and don't include time taken for portage, for lunch breaks, or for scouting. The drop listed is for paddling waters only. It does not include the amount of gradient at dam sites.

Broad River, North and South Carolina

Broad River, North and South Carolina

The Broad, below section (1), winds its way east across southern North Carolina before bending sharply south into South Carolina. Although several dams have been constructed on the river, there are no long stretches of slack water behind them. Total mileage below section (1) is approximately 113 mi.

Topo Maps   Lake Lure, Rutherfordton South, Cowpens, Boiling Springs South, Blacksburg North (N.C.-S.C.); Blacksburg South, Kings Creek, Hickory Grove, Lockhart, Leeds, Carlisle, Blair, Pomaria, Jenkinsville (S.C.)

Counties   Rutherford, Cleveland (N.C.); Cherokee, Union, Newberry (S.C.)

(2)   Rutherford Co. Rt. 1181 bridge to N.C. 108 bridge

Drop	Difficulty	Distance	Time	Scenery	Water Quality
42'	1-2	7 mi.	3 hrs.	A	Good

Gage   None. Runnable year round, except possibly following an extremely long dry spell.

Difficulties   Watch for downed trees. Note: On certain days about halfway down this section those with keen ears may hear the startling scream of the ''Wild Flat Chested Broad Bird,'' although the more discerning paddler of the wild will recognize this unusual sound as the call of the Pea Fowl.

(3)   N.C. 108 bridge to N.C. 1004 bridge

Drop	Difficulty	Distance	Time	Scenery	Water Quality
49'	1-2	9.8 mi.	4 hrs.	A	Good

Gage   None.

Difficulties   None. There are a few riffles on this section, but nothing of any consequence.
Note: The Green River enters on the right .9 mi. above the take out.

Broad River, North and South Carolina

(4) N.C. 1004 bridge to U.S. 221A bridge

Drop	Difficulty	Distance	Time	Scenery	Water Quality
35'	1	13.6 mi.	5.5. hrs.	A	Good

Gage   None.

Difficulties   None.

(5) U.S. 221A bridge to N.C. 150 bridge

Drop	Difficulty	Distance	Time	Scenery	Water Quality
52'	1-2	7.6 mi.	3 hrs.	A-B	Good

Gage   None.

Difficulties   A Duke Power dam is located 1.5 mi. below the put in. Begin moving left after passing under the bridge at the power plant. Pull out on the left just upstream from the cable with drums attached. Carry about 50 yds. to the left, to the bottom of the hill, then parallel the river to an easy put in below the dam (total carry of 150 yds.) Watch the back wash below the dam, being sure to put in well below it. A few small shoals will be encountered occasionally from here on down to N.C. 150.

(6) N.C. 150 bridge to S.C. 18 bridge

Drop	Difficulty	Distance	Time	Scenery	Water Quality
28'	1-2	10.6 mi.	4 hrs.	A-B	Good

Gage   None.

Difficulties   Gaston Shoals or Gravo Dam is reached after some 40 min. of slack water. The dam is constructed in three sections, with the easiest portage to the left of the section on the right (the first section to be approached). Pull out about 30 ft. upstream from the highest concrete. Carry into the small ravine, up to the top and directly down the trail (total carry of 100 yds.) There is an excellent campsite on the right bank below the dam. In low water there will be slow going for some distance below the dam, due to sand deposits.

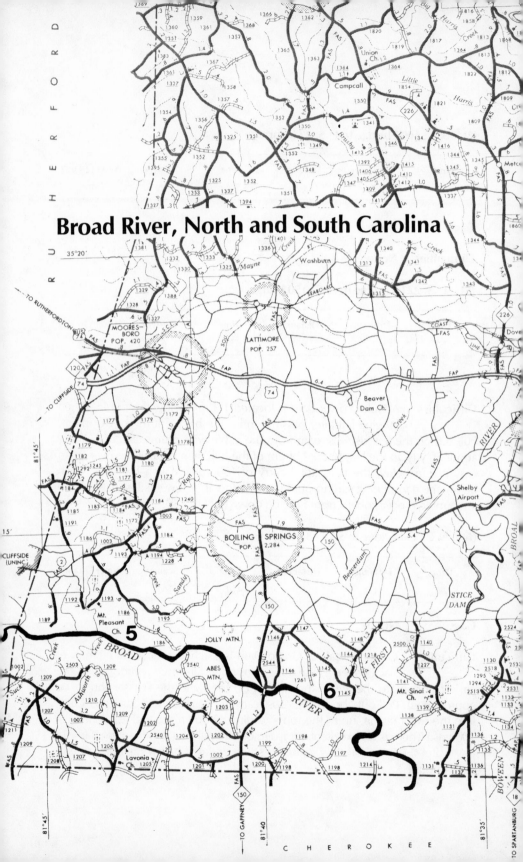

Broad River, North and South Carolina

(7)   S.C. 18 bridge to S.C. 211 bridge

Drop	Difficulty	Distance	Time	Scenery	Water Quality
57'	1-2	17.9 mi.	7 hrs.	A	Good

Gage   None.

Difficulties   Approximately 1 mi. below U.S. 29 bridge there is an area of shoals running for 200 yds., which should be approached rather cautiously—especially at levels even slightly higher than normal. There is a launching ramp on the right at the head of the shoals.

Cherokee Falls Dam is downstream a short distance from the two islands with the old bridge pilings. Water runs over the top, so move to the right as quickly as possible and take out far enough above the dam to prevent being caught by the current. The carry here is fairly short. Following is a series of ledges interspersed among rock gardens, which can prove quite difficult at higher water levels. At normal to lower levels it is best to work to left center and down. Keep to the right channel after the rapids. Note: Cherokee Nuclear Power Plant is a short distance west of the river and some 2 mi. downriver from Cherokee Falls.

There are many large sand bars suitable for camping between Cherokee Falls and the up-coming No. 99 or Ninety-nine Island Dam. It can be recognized by the high, narrow rocky dam on the left. Paddle around the island to the right of this rock dam while staying as close as possible to the island. Bear left around the island and above the face of the dam. Hug it closely for water flows over the dam. Proceed to the left bank, behind the rock dam, to the dock. If the Duke Power staff is on duty, arrangements may be made for a shuttle around the dam and power plant. Otherwise a 600-700 yd. portage along the fence to the side road on the left of the entrance gate and thence down the road to the riverside will be necessary.

(8)   S.C. 211 bridge to Dam at Lockhart

Drop	Difficulty	Distance	Time	Scenery	Water Quality
16'	1	13.6 mi.	5.5 hrs.	A	Good

Gage   None

Difficulties   None until arriving at Lockhart. Move to the extreme right and take out above the log boon. Carry along the fence. The pool

Broad River, North and South Carolina

and sluice running along the right here is closed for any water traffic. There is a distance of 1.4 mi. from here to the next point below the Lockhart Power Company Plant where one can re-enter the river. One alternative, which is questionable as far as ease of accomplishment, is to stay to the left of the dam. This will require a carry through a boulder field below the dam. Paddle the pool below and then carry across the boulders at the opposite end, and paddle the left side of the island from the Power Plant. Whatever the decision, the character building session for the day will begin here and now.

(9)   Lockhart Power Company Powerhouse to S.C. 121 bridge

Drop	Difficulty	Distance	Time	Scenery	Water Quality
27′	1	17.2 mi.	6.5 hrs.	A	Good

Gage   **None**

Difficulties   Neal Shoals Dam is 11 mi. down from Lockhart. Approach on the far left, where a good 60 yd. portage can be made. Watch the slippery rocks! Be sure to put in far enough below the backwash from the dam, and work your way carefully back into the main current. Note: Get permission to drive onto Lockhart Power Company property. Put in about 90 yds. below the power plant at a break in the wall, where a small sand bar is located.

Woods Ferry Recreation Area in Sumter National Forest is 8 mi. below the put in on the east bank. In fact, the National Forest Boundary is just below Lockhart, and the paddle will be within its boundaries down to S.C. 34.

(10)   S.C. 121-72-215 bridge to S.C. 34 bridge

Drop	Difficulty	Distance	Time	Scenery	Water Quality
37′	1-2	15.2 mi.	6 hrs.	A	Good

Gage   None.

Difficulties   There are some riffles along the Shelton Island area (the island is 2 mi. long), the tip of which is located 4 mi. down from the bridge. They aren't difficult, but one may become complacent after a few miles of fairly flat water.

Note: The Tyger enters at 7.4 mi., just above Henderson Island.

Broad River, North and South Carolina

Broad River, North and South Carolina

There are a few shoals immediately above and along Henderson Island. Just below the island an area of shoals extends for close to 200 yds. Approach with caution.

Note: The Enoree enters at 12.4 mi.

Below the Enoree the flow slows appreciably, especially so if power isn't being generated at Parr Shoals. The wind then becomes the only difficulty to be encountered on the remainder of the trip.

Note: Take out at a small launching area about 100 yds. below 34 bridge on the left bank. To reach here, take first right after crossing the bridge going east. Go down the hill and bear hard right across the railroad tracks.

Broad River, North and South Carolina

Enoree River, South Carolina

Enoree River, South Carolina

Enoree River, South Carolina

The Enoree heads up on the Piedmont in Greenville County and winds its way southeasterly to confluence with the Broad, northeast of Newberry. On its way, it cuts through the Fall Line, offering a short stretch of interesting white water before reaching Sumter National Forest and the coastal plains.

From the put in to the take out at Parr Shoals on the Broad, one encounters very little evidence of civilization other than highway bridges. It is a most scenic run through rolling hills.

Topo Maps   Ora, Philson, Crossroads, Sedalia, Whitmire North, Whitmire South, Pomaria, Jenkinsville

Counties   Spartanburg, Union, Newberry

(1)   S.C. 49 bridge to Spartanburg Co. Rt. 10, where it comes alongside the river (.3 mi. above S.C. 56 bridge)

Drop	Difficulty	Distance	Time	Scenery	Water Quality
52'	C-1-2/3	6.8 mi.	3 hrs.	A	Fair

Gage   U.S.G.S. gage is on the east bank 20 yds. above S.C. 49 bridge. Runnable year round. A reading of 3.0 will require a lot of skill and experience to handle the stretch below Rt. 49.

Difficulties   The river drops very quickly within the first .75 mi., with a series of shoals. This fast stretch ends with a drop of some 8 ft. within 100 yds. At higher levels (above 3.0) pull out well above on the left and scout.

(2)   S.C. 56 bridge to Union Co. Rt. 22 bridge

Drop	Difficulty	Distance	Time	Scenery	Water Quality
22'	1	4.5 mi.	2 hrs.	A	Good

Gage   None. Runnable all year. May be a little scratchy following extremely long dry spells.

Difficulties   Downed trees. With water levels following rains extreme care should be taken, expecially with gear-loaded canoes.

Enoree River, South Carolina

(3) Union Co. Rt. 22 bridge to U.S. 176 bridge

Drop	Difficulty	Distance	Time	Scenery	Water Quality
53'	1	17.2 mi.	7 hrs.	A	Good

Gage   None.

Difficulties   See (1).

(4) U.S. 176 bridge to Newberry Co. Rt. 81 bridge

Drop	Difficulty	Distance	Time	Scenery	Water Quality
33'	1	10.4 mi.	4 hrs.	A	Good

Gage   None.

Difficulties   See (2).

(5) Newberry Rt. 81 bridge to S.C. 34 bridge on Broad

Drop	Difficulty	Distance	Time	Scenery	Water Quality
24'	1	12.5 mi.	5.5 hrs.	A	Good

Gage   None.

Difficulties   Winds can become a problem once entering the Broad. If power isn't being generated at Parr Shoals, one will encounter slack water in this area.

(6) S.C. 34 on the Broad to Parr Shoals Dam

Drop	Difficulty	Distance	Time	Scenery	Water Quality
10'	A	10 mi.	5 hrs.	A-B	Good

Gage   None.

Difficulties   Primarily winds. This may become the "character building" part of the trip.

Directions   **Put In**—S.C. 49 bridge west of I-26.

Take Out—Approach the dam (Parr Shoals is the first nuclear power plant in the southeast) on the right, where a graded road runs down and take out. Carry about 100 yds. to the gate. If locked, carry around it. No problem! To drive to the take out go north on S.C. 28 from S.C. 213 for .7 mi. to the first gravel road on the right. Proceed .4 mi. to the gate.

Tyger River, South Carolina

The Tyger is formed in Spartanburg County after the confluence of the North, Middle and South Forks. It then flows generally south and east to meet the Broad east of Whitmire. As it drops through the Fall Line it presents a stretch of rather fast and difficuilt white water before it flattens out in the plains and meanders across Sumter National Forest. Other than the occasional bridges spanning the river, one sees little signs of habitation. The entire stretch is fairly wild and scenic.

Topo Maps   Cross Anchor, Union West, Sedalia, Whitmire North, Blair, Pomaria, Jenkinsville

Counties   Spartanburg, Union, Newberry

(3)   S.C. 56 bridge to S.C. 49 bridge

Drop	Difficulty	Distance	Time	Scenery	Water Quality
38'	1	7 mi.	2.5 hrs.	A	Good

Gage   None. Runnable all year.

Difficulties   Downed trees, although the channel apears to stay fairly clear. Take care at higher than normal levels.

(4)   S.C. 49 bridge to U.S. 176 bridge

Drop	Difficulty	Distance	Time	Scenery	Water Quality
51'	1	11.9 mi.	5 hrs.	A	Good

Gage   None.

Difficulties   See (3). For information: Rose Hill State Park (at S.C. 16) is 4.9 mi. down from the 49 bridge.

(5)   U.S. 176 bridge to Union Co. Rt. 35 bridge

Drop	Difficulty	Distance	Time	Scenery	Water Quality
41'	1	12.7 mi.	5 hrs.	A	Good

Tyger River, South Carolina

Tyger River, South Carolina

Gage   None.

Difficulties   See (3).

(6) Union Co. Rt. 35 and Newberry Co. Rt. 45 bridge to S.C. 34 on the Broad

Drop	Difficulity	Distance	Time	Scenery	Water Quality
25'	1-2	11.6 mi.	4.5 hrs.	A	Good

Gage   None.

Difficulties   After entering the Broad one will hear a rather ominous sound as Henderson Island comes into view. It's only a small shoals extending across the river, but following all the peace and quiet it makes quite a roar. Best passage is probably 20 to 30 ft. off the right bank. There are a few rock gardens on the way down to the end of the island, where shoals run for 150-200 yds. This area should be approached with caution, especially with canoes loaded with gear and inexperienced paddlers.

(7) S.C. 34 bridge to Parr Shoals Dam

Drop	Difficulty	Distance	Time	Scenery	Water Quality
10'	A	10 mi.	5 hrs.	A	Good

Gage   None.

Difficulties   Primarily winds.

Directions   **Take Out**—Approach the dam on the right where a graded road runs down to the water and take out. Carry about 100 yds. to the gate. If locked, carry around it. No problem! To drive to the take out go north on S.C. 28 from S.C. 213 for .7 mi. to first gravel road on right. Proceed .4 mi. to the gate.

Tyger River, South Carolina

Suggested Reading

INSTRUCTIONAL

Basic River Canoeing by Robert McNair   102 pages

American Camping Association, Inc.
Bradford Woods
Martinsbille, Indiana 46151
$3.25

A White Water Handbook for Canoe and Kayak by John Urban   78 pages

Appalachian Mountain Club
5 Joy Street
Boston, Massachusetts 02108
$2.00

The Complete Wilderness Paddler by John Rugge
and James West Davidson   260 pages
Knopf
400 Hahn Road
Westminister, Maryland 21157
$10.00

Pole, Paddle and Portage by Bill Riviere   259 pages

Van Nostrand Reinhold Company
450 West 33rd Street
New York, New York 10001
$7.95

Canoeing by the American Red Cross   452 pages

The best buy for complete canoeing information available. Obtain from
local chapter of American Red Cross.
$3.95

■

. . . an so there ain't nothing more to write about, and I am rotten glad of it, because if I'd'a knowed what a trouble it was to make a book I wouldn't 'a' tackled it, and ain't a-going to no more.

Mark Twain, *from* The Adventures of Huckleberry Finn

'73

It is said that time heals all wounds but I wonder in amazement how in two short years my memory failed to retain the feelings of how the good Mr. Twain had so aptly expressed my sentiments upon completion of the first edition.

—The Author

'76

. . . and here we are again!

—The Author

'80

Index

Stream	Mileage	Page
Alarka Creek	4.5	31
Big Laurel Creek	4.0	71
Broad River	7.4, 112.6	73, 225
Buck Creek	3.2	101
Buffalo Creek	6.0	103
Caney Fork	6.0	33
Catawba River	28.0	105
Catawba, North Fork	5.6	108
Chattooga River	27.0	199
Chauga River	22.7	207
Cullasaja River	5.3	35
Dan River	46.5	171
Davidson River	6.1	75
Deep Creek	2.0	36
Doe River	22.7	209
Elk Creek	8.4	175
Elk River	5.5	213
Enoree River	54.6	237
First Broad River	14.9	76
Fisher River	20.0	176
French Broad River	120.8	79
French Broad, North Fork	7.2	88
Green River	31.9	91
Haw River	12.5	215
Henry Fork	33.1	111
Hiawassee River	22.5	39
Jacob Fork	28.8	115
Johns River	26.0	117
Jonathans Creek	8.8	41
Lewis Fork, North Prong	4.2	178
Lewis Fork, South Prong	3.5	180
Little River	19.9	181
Little Tennessee River	23.0	44
Mayo, North Fork	4.2	184
Mayo, South Fork	5.0	186
Mitchell River	10.5	189
Nantahala River	8.0	46
New River	34.5	121
New River, North Fork	43.0	125
New River, South Fork	89.0	129
Nolichucky River	23.3	135
North Toe and Toe River	65.3	139
North Tyger River	13.8	219

Index

Stream	Mileage	Page
Oconaluftee River	115.0	49
Pigeon River	39.2	51
Pigeon, East Fork	8.7	55
Pigeon, West Fork	6.3	57
Raven Fork	8.0	58
Reddies River	10.0	191
Soco Creek	8.5	60
South Toe River	14.5	145
South Tyger River	5.2	221
South Yadkin River	60.3	148
Stony Fork Creek	6.0	193
Swannanoa River	8.6	95
Tuckaseigee River	45.0	63
Tusquitee River	5.8	69
Tyger River	53.2	219, 241
Upper Creek	11.5	155
Uwharrie River	36.4	157
Watauga River	33.2	161
Wilson Creek	10.4	167
Yadkin River	19.9	195